WELFARE IMPLICATIONS OF DEMOGRAPHIC TRENDS

Tony Fahey
John Fitz Gerald

Oak Tree Press
Dublin
in association with
Combat Poverty Agency

Oak Tree Press
Merrion Building
Lower Merrion Street
Dublin 2, Ireland.

© 1997 Combat Poverty Agency

ISBN 1-86076-053-8

This study forms part of the Combat Poverty Agency's
Research Series, in which it is No. 24. The views
expressed in this report are the authors' own and not
necessarily those of the Combat Poverty Agency.

Printed in Ireland by ColourBooks Ltd.

Contents

Acknowledgements

The authors would like to thank the staff of the Combat Poverty Agency, in particular David Silke, for numerous helpful suggestions and comments which have contributed to this publication. They would also like to thank Anne Vaughan of the Department of Social Welfare and two anonymous referees for very helpful suggestions on earlier drafts. Finally, they would like to thank the staff of the Central Statistics Office for their assistance in extracting additional information from the Labour Force Survey and the Census. The authors alone are responsible for the views expressed in this publication.

Foreword

Introduction

The aim of the Combat Poverty Agency is to work for the prevention and decrease of poverty and social exclusion and the reduction of inequality in Ireland by striving for change which will promote a fairer and more just, equitable and inclusive society. Particularly relevant in this context is its objective to work towards a reduction in existing poverty levels, in particular by promoting the redistribution of income and resources in favour of those living in poverty through reform of the tax and social welfare systems and by working to ensure that everyone has at least a minimally adequate income. Specifically, the Agency is committed to reviewing and analysing the role of income support systems in Ireland in the context of international trends, in particular to examine dependency issues in the social welfare system and to make recommendations on the future direction of the Irish welfare system.

Background to the Research

The Agency commissioned Doctor Tony Fahey and Professor John Fitz Gerald of the Economic and Social Research Institute (ESRI) to undertake this study of the welfare implications of demographic trends. The study was commissioned as part of the Agency's Strategic Plan 1996–1998 and also as a piece of work in its own right to broaden the parameters of the debate on welfare provision. Previous work in this area has tended to focus on the "nuts and bolts" of future welfare demand, broken down by recipient type. This study has tried to move away from that style of demographic projection and instead has focused on the underlying trends that will direct possible future budgetary requirements. This approach has led to a very worthwhile report, which is reader-friendly and which we hope will attract wide discussion, comment and debate among researchers, policy-makers and the general public.

At the core of the study is an examination of the validity of the concern that demographic trends, such as an ageing population and the growth in lone parent numbers, may lead to an unsustainable increase in the level of state support required in Ireland and that this in turn may call into question the affordability of the social welfare system. Such a scenario would have very serious implications for Irish society in general, but particularly for those at risk of or living in poverty.

Policy Implications of Irish Demographic Trends

The report argues that Ireland is now entering an unprecedent d period of demographic advantage. It contends that concerns about the implications of an ageing population are exaggerated in the Irish context over the next twenty years — the time span of the study. The report argues that these concerns are more a "copy-cat" reaction to demographic developments in other countries than based on holistic analysis of Irish population trends. Ireland remains unique, demographically, with any "greying" of the population being counter-balanced by reduced child dependency and increasing female labour force participation.

In addition, the future scenario for Ireland is more positive than it has been in the past when a relatively small productive population has had to support a relatively large dependent population of children, elderly and married women, who although productive in the home were not contributing directly to GNP. The reduction in emigration has also led to an increase in the productive population even though the birth rate has fallen.

A growth in the role of the state in the provision of support for dependants is, however, predicted by the authors. They argue that falling numbers of children and increasing numbers of old people will lead to a shift in support requirements from the family and the market to the state. However, the "greying" of the Irish population will be modest in comparison to other countries. The authors conclude that the Irish state will be able to absorb this increase because of an expansion in the numbers at work and a decline in the numbers unemployed.

Preparing for the Future

In the Agency's view, a constructive approach to preparing for growth in the ageing population is to ensure a continued growth in employment opportunities, thereby widening the tax and social insurance support base from which social provision for older people might be funded. In this regard, the recent Department of Social Welfare's policy document on *Social Insurance in Ireland* (1996), in which the Government's commitment to maintain and develop the social insurance system has been reiterated, is relevant. It will be important that workers' social insurance coverage and entitlements are developed in response to demographic and labour market trends, as demonstrated by the recent ESRI report on pension coverage (Hughes and Whelan, 1996). Also relevant here is the need to review the income support systems in general and the role of universal benefits *vis-à-vis* social insurance *vis-à-vis* social assistance. The European debate on new directions in social welfare and the recent ESRI review of the Commission on Social Welfare's minimum adequate income (Callan *et al.*, 1996a) are important in this regard. Health, housing and social services policies are also relevant in preparing for the growth of an ageing population. The role of carers must also be examined in this context.

Labour Market Opportunities

The authors of the report predict that falling fertility rates will facilitate increased female labour force participation. This, in turn, will contribute to the revenue base from which state social spending is funded. While this seems very plausible it is, however, contingent on the development of adequate, reliable and affordable child-care facilities, which still remain seriously underdeveloped in Ireland. A worrying trend, however, is that it is mainly women who take up the increasing number of part-time, low-paid and non-permanent jobs that are now available. To be sustainable, jobs must provide a decent wage with proper conditions of employment and access to adequate pension coverage. In this context, the implications of the growth in atypical work need to be reviewed.

While it is likely that female labour force participation will continue to increase over the coming years, the implications of the increase in the incidence of lone parenthood (the majority of whom are women) should not be overlooked. In many cases social policy issues for those parenting alone are the same as for two-parent families — for example, adequate child-care and child income support. However, for those parenting alone, the implications of the lack of these services are often more profound than for two-parent families. In addition, young lone parents are particularly vulnerable as they often lack the educational qualifications needed to secure employment and a route out of welfare dependency.

A further issue is the situation of the long-term unemployed, many of whom have not been able to take advantage of the expanding economy. Additional measures in the areas of industrial policy, employment policy, taxation, education and training, and in the social economy are required to ensure that growth in the employment market also provides new opportunities for the long-term unemployed, who will otherwise remain marginalised and excluded.

Education is a Key Resource

The authors of the report make a very interesting link between improved educational levels and changes in demographic trends, such as the fall in fertility and the increase in female labour force participation. Education is the key resource of the next century and one that should be shared more equally. The link between poverty and educational disadvantage is complex but very clear. Overall, children from poorer backgrounds do not perform as well in the education system as their better-off peers. The implications of falling fertility are already working their way through the education system with declining numbers of pupils entering primary school each year. Savings made due to declining numbers of pupils should be redistributed within the education system in favour of those most at risk of educational disadvantage — early school leavers, those at risk of early school leaving and those who are under-performing at school due to poverty. Priority should thus be given to preventing educational disadvantage at an early stage in the educational process by further development of pre-primary and primary interventions and the support of integrated approaches to tackling educational disadvantage.[1]

Contribution to Current Debate

The Agency welcomes this report. It will add greatly to current social, economic and fiscal policy debates about the affordability of adequate welfare payments, priorities in relation to the redistribution of what has now been labelled the "demographic dividend", tax reform, the implications of changes in the distribution of labour market opportunities and the types of opportunities available. The publication of the report is also timely and relevant in the context of the publication of a number of other reports.[2]

The National Anti-Poverty Strategy

This work is also significant in the context of the development of the National Anti-Poverty Strategy. This strategy, which was initiated in response to the Government's commitment at the UN Social Summit in Copenhagen in 1995, will ensure that all government departments and state agencies include the reduction and prevention of poverty as key objectives in the development and implementation of their policies and programmes. The strategy has been developed on the basis of five themes: educational

---

[1] In 1996, the Agency initiated a Demonstration Programme on Educational Disadvantage which is running in four Area Partnerships for three years. The programme focuses on the development and modelling of locally driven, integrated responses to educational disadvantage to inform policy and practice nationally (see Howley, J., "New Pathways to Tackling Educational Disadvantage", *Poverty Today*, No. 31, March/April 1996, Combat Poverty Agency).

[2] See, in particular: *Review of the Commission on Social Welfare's Minimum Adequate Income* (Callan *et al.*, 1996a), *Poverty in the 1990s* (Callan *et al.*, 1996b), *Report of the Expert Group on the Integration of the Tax and Social Welfare Systems* (1996), the Department of Social Welfare's discussion paper on *Social Insurance in Ireland* (1996), the Forfás report on *Shaping our Future — A Strategy for Enterprise in Ireland in the 21st Century* (1996), the NESC report on a *Strategy into the 21st Century* (1996), IBEC's report on *Social Policy in a Competitive Economy* (1996) and research on *Occupational and Personal Pension Coverage* (Hughes and Whelan, 1996).

disadvantage, income adequacy, unemployment, urban concentrations of poverty and rural poverty.

This report on the social welfare implications of demographic trends provides valuable information on the wider picture in which the strategy will operate. It gives a positive indication that, if there is a political commitment to tackle poverty, Irish demographic trends are ripe for positive change to reduce substantially current levels of poverty and inequality in Ireland. Opportunities such as these are rare and their potential must be recognised and harnessed.

Partnership 2000

The new national programme *Partnership 2000 for Inclusion, Employmer.t and Competitiveness* provides an important context in which Irish policy will be developed over the next three years. While not explicitly referring to demographic trends, it identifies three essential economic and social challenges. These are:

- maintaining an effective and consistent policy approach in a period of high economic growth;

- significantly reducing social disparities and exclusion, especially by reducing long-term unemployment; and

- responding effectively, at national, sectoral and enterprise level, to global competition and the information society.

Given the demographic trends presented in this report, the period 1997–1999 thus offers Government and the social partners a unique opportunity to make major inroads on the issues of poverty, unemployment and social exclusion in Ireland and to meet the challenges presented in the *Partnership 2000* programme.

European Union Context

While it is important to view the welfare implications of demographic trends in an Irish context, it is also sensible to set these in the broader European context. The European dimension will play a crucial role in the Irish situation over the next number of years as the Irish economy is affected by larger member states' fiscal and monetary policies. In particular, the development of a European Monetary System (EMS) will have significant effects on how the national position progresses. Also critical for Ireland in an EU context is the expansion of the membership of the EU and the next period of structural funds (post-1999). The level of resources may not be as substantial as previously, and Ireland may no longer be able to rely on the extent of current Structural Funds to redress imbalances. However, it should be remembered that this is in the context of Ireland's favourable demographic and economic projections. Thus it is crucial that resource allocation in the areas of employment, income support, education, health and housing are maintained and increased if Ireland is to avoid higher levels of poverty and social exclusion.

Concluding Remarks

In conclusion, this report brings into clear focus the key policy issues and options for the next twenty years. These years will be marked not by growing dependency but by a demographic dividend, which we must now plan to use to benefit those experiencing poverty and social exclusion. In particular, these resources should be used to tackle the persistent scourge of family poverty caused by inadequate income, educational disadvantage and lack of access to the labour market. Urgent attention must be paid to the development of support mechanisms — for instance, by making social welfare rates adequate, by further development of policies for the long-term unemployed, by investing more resources in child-care and by improving social services for the elderly, particularly those living in rural areas. Social solidarity now will sustain economic competitiveness in the future by increasing labour force participation and reducing welfare costs. Ireland, therefore, has a unique opportunity in the years ahead to secure economic and social viability. In essence, we have the capacity, if we have the will, to tackle the endemic problems of unemployment, poverty and social exclusion.

It should be noted that this report deals solely with the welfare implications of demographic trends. A complementary study for further research could be to explore economic projections for industrial policy and the supply of employment, in particular the types of jobs being provided and the sustainability of those and existing jobs.

Finally, the Agency would like to thank Tony Fahey and John Fitz Gerald for their work and to congratulate them on a very well researched and very readable report. We would also like to thank all those who commented on earlier drafts of the report. In particular, the Agency would like to thank Patricia O'Hara of Callaghan Associates and Gerry O'Hanlon of the Central Statistics Office, whose contributions were vital in setting the project on a sound footing. We would also like to thank officials from the Department of Social Welfare and the Department of Finance and anonymous referees, who commented on the final draft of the report.

Combat Poverty Agency
January 1997

Chapter 1

Introduction

Background

Over recent years, concern has been voiced in many developed countries that certain demographic trends, especially rapid population ageing, pose a threat to economic growth and more particularly to the affordability of existing social welfare systems (see, for example, World Bank, 1994; OECD, 1988). A large elderly population, it is argued, is likely to make pension and social security systems excessively expensive and may lead to a "war of the generations", with older people, workers and children struggling over the distribution of economic resources.

These concerns have been rejected by others. The demographic analyses which have given rise to them have been criticised by some as simplistic and alarmist (Schulz *et al.*, 1991; Guillemard, 1991). Others have accused agencies such as the World Bank of causing a false scare about the public expenditure implications of demographic trends as part of a neo-liberal attack on the welfare state (Johnson, 1996; Lloyd-Sherlock, 1996; Vincent, 1996). A range of alternative and less pessimistic views on the effects of present population trends on the economy and welfare systems have been offered. These include the argument that population trends, however significant in themselves, are not major determinants of welfare expenditure — changes in the structure of the welfare system, economic development, contests between competing interests groups, and developments in policy are all likely to be more influential (Guillemard, 1991). A somewhat different argument is that an isolated focus on population ageing, and especially on the elderly as a component of that trend, which has characterised much of the literature on the "demographic threat" in developed countries, is likely to be misleading. It is necessary also to take account of additional factors such as the decline in the child population, the possible future fall in unemployment and continued growth in economic productivity to get a proper picture. These developments, it is suggested, could well counterbalance any negative effects on the economy or on the welfare state which might arise from an increase in the population of older people, and could therefore mean that population dependency burdens in the future are likely to remain at levels similar to or below those which prevailed in the past (Schulz *et al.*, 1991).

The debates which have taken place on these questions indicate that demographic issues have assumed a new importance in discussions about future economic development, and especially about the future of the welfare state. They also demonstrate, however, that there is no consensus as to the impact these trends might have. As a recent review by the European Commission concludes, there is general agreement that further population ageing now seems inevitable, but no agreement whatever on the consequences this trend will have on economic growth and public expenditure (European Commission, 1994).

The Demographic Situation in Ireland

These debates in other countries have had some influence in Ireland and have given rise to some gloomy predictions about the pressures on the Irish economy and state expenditure arising from demographic trends, especially population ageing (see, for example, National Pensions Board, 1993, especially pp. 37–47). In noting such predictions, we should first recall the lack of consensus in international research about the impact of demographic trends in these areas. Even in countries where population ageing is already well advanced, it is not at all clear what the consequences have been or whether the negative predictions are coming to pass.

In addition, it is even more important to recall that, despite the convergence of certain demographic indicators on the European norm in recent years, the demographic situation in Ireland is still quite exceptional. This is so for a number of reasons. One is the record of population decline which prevailed in Ireland until the 1960s and still leaves its mark on Ireland's population structures today. Heavy emigration was one of the key components of that poor long-term record. The emigration surge of the 1950s in particular drained off a large portion of the young-adult cohort of that period, and population structures in Ireland have not yet fully recovered from that haemorrhage. Much of the loss occurred among those now in their fifties and early sixties, the leadership-age cohort of today. It undoubtedly debilitated that age cohort in numbers, entrepreneurial talent and leadership ability, to the detriment of economic, social and political life right up to today. (Mjoset (1992) places emigration at the centre of his explanation for Ireland's poor economic performance in the present century.)

Low marriage rates were another feature of Ireland's poor population performance, with the consequence that among those who remained single, many were left stranded without family networks as they aged. For those who did marry fertility remained high. However, because of the combined effects of mortality and emigration, large shares of each birth cohort were lost to the population in childhood or early adulthood. As a result, population reproduction was usually well below replacement levels. Below-replacement fertility rates may well be a new feature of population patterns in Ireland and in western countries as a whole in recent years, but a more general failure to replace population was a persistent characteristic of Irish population performance between 1850 and 1960.

The limited degree of population recovery which has emerged since the 1960s occurs against this background of longer term decline and poor reproductive performance. That recovery has by no means eliminated the consequences of the earlier record, but it has introduced a new dynamic into Irish population structures. While this new dynamic in some ways brings Ireland closer into line with the experience of other countries, in other ways its peculiar timing and nature serves to keep Ireland on a distinctive trajectory. The Irish "baby boom" occurred in the 1970s and early 1980s, considerably later than the baby boom of the late 1940s or 1950s which occurred in most other western countries. The baby-boom generation in Ireland, therefore, is now in late adolescence and early adulthood rather than middle age — it is about 30 years younger than the baby boom generation of North America or western Europe. Fertility has fallen sharply since the early

1980s, so that the generation now in childhood, which will be reaching the brink of adulthood in about 15 years time, is likely to be small in numbers. Even then, however, the preceding generation — the baby boom generation of the 1970s and early 1980s — will still be in their prime years (30s and 40s) so that the overall population profile in the early decades of the next century will still be quite vigorous. Furthermore, falling emigration means that reproductive efficiency is likely to be greatly increased — fewer children will not necessarily translate into fewer adults, since the haemorrhage of emigration is likely to be much lower than in the past. In the context of Ireland's unique population history, a low-fertility/low-emigration regime could well be healthier in social and economic terms than the high-fertility/high-emigration regime which was so characteristic of the past.

As well as being out of step with other countries in the timing of its fertility trends, Ireland has had a distinctively poor record in the extension of older people's life expectancy. Ireland's principal public health achievement since the 1940s has been in the sharp reduction of infant and early adult mortality rather than in extensions to later life. As a result, increased longevity at older ages has not been as significant an influence on population structure as in other countries and has dampened the tendency towards population ageing (Fahey and Murray, 1994). Furthermore, the present-day legacy of emigration in the 1950s means that the generation now on the verge of old age is disproportionately small and provides a comparatively limited base for growth in the numbers of older people in the short- to medium-term future. In those countries where population ageing represents a problem, it is a problem which arises from past success in boosting fertility, reducing mortality (especially at older ages) and absorbing consequent population growth. Ireland has been notably lacking in those successes in the past and is similarly lacking in the consequences arising from them today.

Most western countries are now coming out of a long-sustained upswing in demographic performance and have to adjust to the after-effects of long-term demographic expansion. Ireland, by contrast, is still emerging from a long trough and is now in a relatively strong position. Irish population structure, both now and for the next 10–20 years, is less top-heavy with older people than is the case in other western countries and is relatively better endowed with people in or on the brink of the productive age-ranges. It has a smaller child population than it had in the past, but that population segment is still reasonably large by the standards of many other countries. More importantly in the light of Irish population history, larger numbers of today's children are likely to find a place as adults in Ireland than was the case for most cohorts of children in the present century.

Together, these factors mean that, in certain basic ways, Irish population structure is now in an usually favourable condition, particularly in comparison with its own past. Furthermore, the favourable features in Irish demographic patterns are now only in their incipient stages. They are likely to come to full fruition over the next three decades and mean that the *direction* of present trends is more favourable than in other western countries. Because of the recent fall in the fertility rate, the situation may become less favourable as the bulk of the baby-boom generation enters old age from the mid-2020s onwards. However, this eventuality is three or four decades down the road, and even then it may be less burdensome in its impact than the demographic problems of the recent past. As we note below, even short-term forecasts are often inaccurate. Long-term projections are much more liable to wide error and should be treated circumspectly on that account. It is more fruitful to concentrate on the general shape and impact of events in the short- to medium-term future and not to become excessively concerned about developments which may or may not lie beyond distant horizons.

Demographic Weaknesses

While present Irish population structures warrant a great deal of optimism, they nevertheless do have problems of their own. The central problem is the same as that which has dogged Irish population structures since the mid-nineteenth century — the almost continuous inability of Irish society to absorb each generation as it reaches adulthood. Apart from a short period in the late 1960s and early 1970s, no generation has been able to find a full place in adult society for anything approaching all of its members. In previous generations, this problem was reflected in a uniquely high rate of emigration — the dispersal abroad of the "surplus" young adult population. Today, the emigration tide has been stemmed by the stagnant condition of our usual foreign labour markets, so that the absorption problem has stayed at home and accumulated in the form of the 250,000 or so adults who are either unemployed or seriously underemployed.[1] The scale and persistence of this problem means that, although we have relatively large numbers of people in the productive age ranges, both now and for the medium-term future, a large number of those people are not in fact productive. Instead of contributing to the support of the dependent segments of the population, they themselves become dependent. The forms of dependency they experience, particularly in the case of those who are long-term unemployed, are especially psychologically damaging to themselves, have knock-on social effects in the wider community and form a large drain on welfare resources. In considering present and future welfare requirements in Ireland, therefore, trends in the size and characteristics of this group will assume greater importance than in most other countries.

A number of other trends have also often been cited as sources of concern for the future. These include the growth in the incidence of lone parenthood and the growth in the size of the elderly population. While these trends do not merit much of the alarmist comment which they sometimes attract, they nevertheless amount to serious developments which need to be taken into account.

---

[1] Precise, comprehensive measures of the extent of unused or underused labour in Ireland are not available. Counts of the unemployed provide a major portion of such a measure, but there is a difficulty in deciding between the Live Register and the Labour Force Survey as the best such count. While the Labour Force Survey may be the best measure of unemployment in a strict sense, the Live Register, despite its inaccuracies, may be a better indicator of the numbers who are not fully self-supporting in economic terms. An equally serious problem is the lack of information on the nature and extent of underemployment — for example, among certain categories of the self-employed (such as small farmers or proprietors of small businesses) or among women in the home who are deterred from seeking paid work by the poor state of labour demand.

Objectives and Layout of Study

The purpose of the present study is to examine the likely impact of future demographic trends on welfare and income support requirements in Ireland, taking account of the peculiar demographic circumstances which prevail in Ireland. It aims in particular to assess the interactions between different aspects of demographic trends — such as the decline in the numbers of children combined with the increase in the numbers of older people — as influences on welfare and support requirements.

The scope of the study is limited in a number of ways. It does not attempt to develop a formal quantitative model of the support system which might be used to project the outcome of the interactions it points to. Rather, it confines itself to a discursive assessment of what the most obvious of those interactions involve. It deals only with the numerically large categories of dependency (children, the unemployed, the elderly) and so does not refer to smaller groups such as the disabled or the mentally ill. Finally, it deals only with dependency and support patterns at the national level and so does not consider the important question of regional or urban–rural variations. While these are significant limitations, we feel that they are not so substantial as to negate the study or to undermine the broad thrust of the conclusions it arrives at.

In pursuing its objectives, the first step in the study is to consider the issues and concepts which underlie the analysis: what is meant by demographic dependency and the support requirements which go with it; how these are linked to the details of population structure; how the *kinds* of support as well as the overall level of support which are required may be influenced by demographic factors. The discussion of these issues is the subject of Chapter 2.

In Chapter 3, utilising the definitions and measures set out in Chapter 2, the report turns to an account of dependency trends in Ireland, referring especially to the actual record over the last 30 years and the forecast for the next 30 years.

Chapters 4, 5 and 6 focus in turn on a detailed analysis of certain component changes within the overall trends. Chapter 4 deals with changes in the level and composition of fertility and marriage, in so far as is possible with the limited data available. Chapter 5 examines labour force participation and focuses on trends in the educational composition of the population, an issue which falls outside of demography in the narrow sense but which nevertheless is a central aspect of present and future changes in Irish population patterns. Chapter 6 examines the extent and implications of population ageing.

Chapter 7 pulls together the main findings of the report and draws out the implications for welfare policy.

Accuracy and Scope of Projections

It should be noted that the present study, like any analysis based on demographic projections, rests on uncertain foundations since demographic forecasting is such an uncertain exercise. Strictly speaking, demographic projections are largely hypothetical in that they say, "if certain trends continue, this is what will happen in the future". They are empirically accurate to the extent that they reflect where we are headed *now* (or rather, where we were headed at the date of the most recently available demographic data, which, in the Irish case, can be 2–3 years earlier than the date the projections are made). But they do not allow for the sharp bends which are almost bound to occur in the road ahead, and in any event are highly sensitive to the precise aspects of recent trends which are selected as the bases for projections into the future.

Past experience has shown not only that population projections often diverge from each other[2] but also that actual developments commonly diverge from what the projections forecast within a short time of the projections being made (Fahey, 1995, pp. 16–19). The projections on which the present report is based — those produced by the Central Statistics Office (CSO) in 1995 (CSO, 1995) — have already suffered that fate. The preliminary report for the 1996 Census of Population (CSO, 1996) shows that population performance between 1991 and 1996 was better than had been expected, largely because migration showed a small net inflow (3,800) over the period in place of the 35,000 net outflow which had been assumed in the CSO's 1995 projections. Total population

---

[2] See Chapter 6 (pp. 85–88) for some comparisons between projections of population and labour force trends published in recent years.

in 1996 turned out to be almost 1 per cent greater than the higher of the projections made by the CSO in 1995. Those projections assumed that net emigration would continue to be substantial up to 2006, an assumption which may have been reasonable then but now seems less likely. If those projections were to be re-done now, the forecasts would be revised upwards, to the extent that the upper bound estimates made in 1995 might well become the lower bound estimates now. Furthermore, given the rapid convergence of Ireland's living standards on the EU average, it is now beginning to appear plausible to consider that Ireland might experience long-term net *inward* migration in the future, a possibility which has never yet been incorporated into any population projection model for Ireland. The CSO's 1995 projections also made projections of the labour force up to 2006. Until labour force estimates for 1996 become available it is not yet possible to judge the short-term accuracy of these projections. However, if they are in error, it is likely to be on the side of caution rather than of optimism (compare, for example, the optimistic note on employment and the labour force in the ESRI's *Quarterly Economic Commentary*, September 1996; see also Chapter 6).

These observations are not intended as criticisms of the CSO's 1995 projections, but as reminders of the impossibility of providing wholly reliable forecasts of population and labour force trends, even over the short term. The implication is, first, that we should not be overly concerned about the precise figures provided in the projections. The projections should be used as indicators of general trends, and even at that may get things wrong. A second implication is that, whatever value projections have for the short to medium term, they have much less value for the long term, even when the focus is on the general direction of trends. It would be unwise to attach too much policy significance to long-term forecasts, for example, by adopting policy stances now on the bases of the population or labour force for the year 2026 or later.[3]

---

[3] The Final Report of the National Pensions Board, *Developing the National Pensions System* (National Pensions Board, 1993) takes a more liberal view of what is possible with demographic forecasts than what we suggest here. It makes population and labour force projections up to the year 2035 as a basis for forecasts of the future pension demand and the capacity of present financ-

We should also recall that certain sub-aggregates are extremely difficult to forecast, even though they may have great interest for policy purposes. This is particularly true of the labour force and associated sub-aggregates such as the employed and unemployed. These are shaped by a range of factors such as migration, participation rates and trends in labour demand which are difficult to predict individually beyond a few years and which cannot be usefully projected in interaction with each other for the long-term future. It is for this reason that the CSO's 1995 projections make labour force forecasts only up to 2006 (rather than to 2026 as in the case of population) and, within the labour force, do not disaggregate into the employed and unemployed. Similarly, the ESRI's periodic *Medium Term Review* does not project labour force or employment totals for more than fifteen years ahead, and even at that would consider estimates for the later portion of such projection periods as quite conjectural. It is possible to forecast such sub-aggregates as employment and unemployment up to, say, 2020 or even 2035 but in practice such projections would be too speculative to be useful for policy.

Because of the disappearance of net emigration since 1991, combined with falling unemployment and rapid labour force growth since 1993, revised projections currently being prepared in the ESRI are likely to forecast stronger growth in population, the labour force and the numbers at work up to 2011 than do the projections used in the present report. These revisions will principally affect the support base for welfare provision (the active ranges and the labour force) and will have fewer implications, in the short to medium term at least, for existing forecasts of the dependent age-ranges. The results of these revisions are not yet available and cannot be incorporated into the present study. It should be kept in mind, however, that they are likely to be somewhat more positive about the future outlook for Ireland on these issues than is the already positive picture set out in the present study.

---

ing arrangements to meet the costs associated with that demand. It draws a number of policy conclusions from this exercise. The validity and usefulness of doing so is critically assessed in Chapter 6 below.

Chapter 2

Conceptual Framework

Introduction

This chapter deals with the conceptual issues which arise in examining the links between population trends and changes in welfare and support requirements. It focuses firstly on how the concept of dependency may be defined and measured. It then considers the different kinds of support which link the dependent with the productive sectors of the population and which may be affected by changes in population structure.

Dependency — Concept and Measurement

Dependency and Population Structure

In examining the implications of population change for welfare and support requirements, the starting assumption is that all human populations consist of some who are dependent, in that they cannot produce sufficient output to support themselves, and others who not only produce enough to support themselves but also, to varying degrees, generate a surplus which, in principle at least, is capable of meeting the needs of those who are dependent. The composition and relative size of the dependent and productive segments of the population determine its dependency level. Dependency level thus defined can be quantified in various ways, most simply by establishing the numerical balance which exists between the dependent and productive population segments — how many dependants there are per producer. Support requirements can be deduced in a general way from dependency levels, thus completing the link between population patterns and questions of support and welfare.

The division of populations into dependent and productive segments is, of course, a simplification. Dependence and productivity are two ends of a continuum rather than two sides of a clearly evident boundary. At one end of this continuum are the highly productive workers who generate output far beyond their own needs, in the centre are those who produce enough to support themselves but no others, and at the other end are those (such as small children or extremely dependent elderly) who are completely unable to support themselves. Furthermore, the continuum has breadth as well as length: at each point along the way, one will find different kinds of production or dependence, though it may be difficult to grade them in a consistent manner. Thus, while a year-old infant and a 75-year old with Alzheimer's disease may both be extremely dependent, their support needs may be so different as to make it difficult to say how similar or different their dependency levels are. Likewise, a housewife looking after a family and the average industrial worker are both productive. However, they differ greatly in the nature, and possibly in the level, of their productivity and it would be difficult to establish fully how similar or different their productivity is.

Nevertheless, despite the simplification involved in dividing the populations into the dependent and the productive, the underlying idea has a strong appeal, if only because it is both easily grasped and easily quantified. The measures which result, though crude, can be helpful in thinking about the welfare implications of demographic trends. It is possible to try to correct for at least some of the distortions which might arise from the more simplistic methods of measuring dependency levels, thus giving them a greater degree of realism. This is particularly so where, as is usually the case, the focus is on trends over time rather than on levels at any given time. Some of the distortions which arise in measuring dependency may recur in more or less consistent fashion from one period in time to the next. Thus, they may have little impact on the accuracy of the trend estimates, however much they distort estimates of levels at the various points along the way.

Age-dependency Ratios

The simplest and most widely used measure of the dependency level of a population is the age-dependency ratio. This is the ratio between children and old people on the one hand (those in the "dependent" age ranges) and the "active" population on the other. In this context, children are conventionally defined as those aged under 15 and the elderly as those aged 65 and over. The active population is the residual, those aged 15–64. "Young dependency" is the ratio of children to the active population, "old dependency" is the ratio of the elderly to the active population, and total dependency is the sum of the young and old dependency.

Age-dependency ratios have the advantage of being easy to understand and simple to compute. They give a crude indication of the changing balance between dependent and productive segments of the population in the course of common demographic changes — for example, during rises or declines in fertility (which cause the number of children to expand or contract), or increases in life expectancy at older ages (which causes the elderly population to expand). They are thus used as a common shorthand for measuring changes in dependency levels in a population over time, as well as for comparing dependency levels between populations.

However, as indicators of support requirements, age-dependency ratios are based on a number of simplifying assumptions, at least some of which can be improved upon to enhance the realism of the measures. Two of these assumptions in particular will concern us here. One relates to the relative dependency of children and old people. Age-dependency ratios assume that children and old people have more-or-less identical dependency levels, so that changes in the child population have the same significance as changes in the size of the elderly population in determining overall dependency. We need to consider if this is a reasonable assumption. The second issue is that many of those aged 15–64 are not economically productive — e.g. the unemployed, those in full-time education, those in early retirement, the long-term ill or disabled. It clearly distorts matters to treat these categories as part of the productive population. A more realistic approach is to isolate those in the active age ranges who are in fact economically productive and treat the rest of the population as dependent.

There are many additional issues which one could consider in attempting to go beyond age-dependency ratios as measures of dependency, such as the extent of hidden productive activity among children and old people. However, an adequate treatment of these and many similar issues would require a more thorough approach than is possible in the present report. For present purposes, therefore, we will consider only the two issues mentioned.

Children's and Old People's Dependency Compared

Usually, total age-dependency ratios are computed simply as the sum of young and old dependency ratios and no allowance is made for the possibility that children and old people may have different dependency levels. Clearly, however, it is possible that children may require either more or less support than older people, in which case an appropriate weighting ought to be applied to age-dependency ratios to improve their adequacy as measures of support requirements.

Little research has been devoted to the question of the relative support requirements of children and old people. Dependency has been examined for children and old people separately, but few attempts have been made to standardise the estimates for the two groups so as to make them comparable. In so far as the question is addressed at all, the tendency is to conclude that children are "cheaper" than old people. For example, in order to weight the dependency levels of children and old people, Cutler *et al.* (1990) examine private non-medical consumption, medical care and public education by age-group. They attach an overall weight of 0.72 to people under 20, of 1 to people aged 21–64 and 1.27 to those aged 65 and over. This implies that old people require 1.8 times more support than children. This weighting has been adopted by OECD researchers as a "first approximation" to calculating needs-weighted support ratios for the OECD as a whole (Leibfritz *et al.*, 1995, pp. 54, 58).

Apportioning either private or public expenditures to age-groups is fraught with difficulty so that any estimates along the lines proposed by Cutler and his colleagues have to be treated with caution. However, there is an additional major difficulty with such estimates which greatly reduces their value for present purposes. They focus on financial expenditures on children, both private and public, in comparison with financial expenditures on other age groups. They thus take no account of the *indirect cost of informal family care.* This is particularly important in the present context not only because children are enormous consumers of informal personal care but also because they are much heavier consumers of such care than are old people. The indirect or hidden costs associated with informal care have wide ramifications since they affect such things as women's labour force participation and thus have consequences for the size of the tax base which is available to fund formal state services. A focus on financial expenditures to the exclusion of informal care thus understates the cost of children both absolutely and in comparison with the cost of elderly people.

No attempts have been made in Ireland to estimate the extent or economic value of informal childcare by mothers or other family members. However, an indication of the scale of what is involved can be gleaned from labour force data on the deployment of mothers' labour. In Ireland in 1992, there were 427,000 mothers with children under the age of 15, of whom 263,000 (62 per cent) were outside the labour force (*Labour Force Survey,* 1992). We do not know what share of their waking hours the mothers of dependent children devote to childcare, but it is likely to be quite large, even for those with jobs outside the home. In aggregate, the total quantum of time involved is likely to be enormous and to be the equivalent of a significant share of GNP.

In those countries where attempts have been made to isolate the childcare component of unpaid housework and value it, uncertainties exist over the precise amounts of time involved and over the economic value to be placed on that time. Haveman and Wolfe (1995), for example, provide a lower bound estimate of the cost of children to families in the United States at $13,515 per child, which in aggregate translates into 14.5 per cent of GDP. Of this amount, $1,693 per child, or 12.5 per cent of the total, is accounted for by the opportunity cost of mother's childcare time (it is assumed for the lower bound estimate that fathers devote no time to childcare). This lower bound estimate, however, is based on the assumption that women work only 40 hours per week. Childcare time per woman is calculated as the difference between their actual time at paid work and 40 hours per week (on that basis, mothers who work 40 hours per week are assumed to spend no time caring for their children). At the other extreme, Haveman and Wolfe derive an upper bound estimate by assuming that mothers devote an average of 38 hours per week to childcare and by adding in a component for fathers' childcare. On that basis, the total annual cost per child rises to $32,000 per year, or 34 per cent of GDP, of which $20,000 is accounted for by the cost of parents' time (Haveman and Wolfe, 1995, p. 1831).

In short, these estimates suggest that the cost of informal family care per child in the United States falls somewhere between $1,693 and $20,000 per year — meaning that it could account for between one-eighth and three-quarters of the total cost of children. While the large gap between the upper and lower bound estimates reflects the difficulty in computing the full cost of children, the amounts involved even at the lower edge indicate that informal family care is a major component of the total cost of children.

The majority of old people, by contrast, are largely free of the personal care needs which characterise childhood. About one-fifth of elderly people living in the community depend on others (usually family members) for some form of personal assistance or care — meaning that four out of five require no such care (Larragy, 1993; O'Shea and Hughes, 1994; Fahey and Murray, 1994, pp. 126–7). Among the very dependent elderly, it appears that the majority are cared for in institutions rather than in their own homes (Larragy, 1993, p. 363). For those who do receive care at home, the amount of time involved on the part of the care provider varies greatly. It can be very high in the case of care provided by family members co-residing with very dependent elderly, though these account for only a minority of those receiving care (Larragy, 1993). At the other extreme, among elderly people who received help with daily tasks from persons living outside their households (usually family members but sometimes also paid home-helps), the median amount of time involved was between five and six hours per week (data from ESRI's *Survey of the Over 65s*, 1993). Furthermore, a portion of personal care for the frail elderly is provided either through social services or private market services (for example, in the form of home helps or nursing home care) and so is accounted for in the formal economy. A further large portion is provided by other elderly persons, especially spouses, for whom the opportunity cost of time is likely to be less than is the case for parents of young children who might otherwise be in paid work.

In sum, informal family care is not as universal a requirement for older people as it is for children, it reaches high levels (similar to those for infants) only among small minorities of old people, and often has lower opportunity cost than care of young children by their parents. Informal care is therefore likely to be a much smaller component of the total per capita cost of older people than it is for the corresponding cost of children. Thus, while the *formal* cost of older people, as expressed in private and public expenditure combined, may be greater than the formal cost of children (as per the Cutler *et al.* estimates quoted above), the balance is reversed in the case of *informal* costs.

It is impossible in the present state of knowledge in Ireland to quantify and compare these costs for children and older people. Nevertheless, taking account of the full picture outlined above, one could make a reasonable working assumption that, taking all costs together — public and private, financial and non-financial, formal and informal — children and old people probably require broadly similar levels of support. Certainly, there is no clear justification for considering that children cost *less* than old people, as is usually done. Rather, as far as the measurement of overall dependency levels are concerned, the most reasonable approach would seem to be *not* to introduce needs-related weightings of young and old dependency ratios. The standard practice of simply summing the unweighted ratios to arrive at a total age-dependency ratio would probably be the more realistic approach.

There may be a case in certain circumstances for using needs-related weights — for example, if the concern is to examine support requirements which operate through the formal economy rather than the total support requirement. It would be important in such cases, however, to be clear about the limited application of the support measures which result. In Chapter 3, we will indicate what a needs-weighted dependency ratio looks like in the Irish case (using the weightings advanced by Cutler *et al.* (1990)) and how it diverges from the total age-dependency ratio. However, this will be for illustrative purposes rather than to suggest that needs-weighting of support ratios is a necessary adjustment to make.

Economic Dependency

The second problem with age-dependency ratios which we are concerned with is that large numbers of those in the active age range of 15–64 are economically dependent. The largest such categories are those in full-time education, principally in the age range 15–24, the unemployed and those in early retirement. While there are undoubtedly many borderline cases in each of these groups (students with part-time jobs, nominally unemployed people who work in the black economy, etc.), the simplest adjustment is to restrict the definition of the productive category to those at work and to treat the other groups as uniformly dependent. Economic dependency could thus be defined as the ratio between the numbers at work and the rest of the population.

This leaves one remaining uncertainty — how to treat those engaged in home duties. This is a category which is overwhelmingly comprised of women. In Ireland, in contrast with most other developed societies, this category is still very large (the participation of married women in the labour force in Ireland, though rising, is still low by international standards — about 39 per cent according to the 1995 *Labour Force Survey*). While women working in the home are normally defined as economically inactive, they in fact make a large economic contribution through housework and childcare. In fact, as discussed in the previous section, the opportunity cost of women's time working in the home is one of the main components in the support requirements of children. Women engaged in that capacity belong to the productive categories of the population even if they do not take part in formal paid work. In computing the economic dependency ratio, therefore, there is a strong case to be made that women in full-time home duties should be counted alongside those in formal paid work to arrive at the total of those at work.

On the other hand, given the poor level of labour demand in the paid economy in Ireland, it is likely that many women in home duties form a reservoir of hidden unemployment or underemployment — they are not fully occupied by their work in the home and would seek and take paid employment if it were available. Thus, while it would greatly understate the size of the productive population to omit housewives altogether (as is usually done), it might overstate the productive population somewhat to assume that all housewives were fully productive in housework.

It is worth noting too that, in addition, even for those women in the home for whom housework and childcare is a genuinely full-time job, the work they perform takes place in the informal economy. While this does not reduce the value of such work nor its significance as a form of support to dependent segments of the population, it has the important characteristic that it places the returns to such work outside the income tax net. Housework does not yield income tax revenues to the state.

In addition, because of the system of tax-free allowances for married couples which now prevails in Ireland, married women in the home give rise to significant tax expenditures, in the form of tax-free allowances for non-working spouses. Callan and Farrell (1991) indicate the scale of the tax expenditure involved by calculating the extra tax revenues to the state which would arise if spouses were to be taxed on *almost* the same basis as two single persons — that is, where a portion of a non-working spouse's tax allowances would be transferable to the working spouse, in place of the full transferability of both tax free allowances and tax bands which is in place at present. They arrive at a conservative estimate of £350 million in extra revenue to the state in 1991 from such a reform of the tax system (Callan and Farrell, 1991, p. 90). This estimate of the tax-cost to the state of married women working in the home does not imply that housewives should be treated as dependent rather than productive, but it does alert us to the implications for the type of support provided which arise from housework as opposed to other kinds of productive activity.

In Chapter 3 we will make some attempt to incorporate these concerns about housework into the computation of economic dependency ratios. However, since we will be concerned with future as well as past economic dependency, these efforts will be hampered by a lack of forecasts on the future numbers of women in home duties. CSO projections, for example, give forecasts on the future size of the labour force but, among the economically "inactive" population, they make no forecasts of the breakdown between home duties and other forms of "inactivity" (full-time education, retirement, etc.). Therefore, it is not possible to incorporate future estimates of the numbers in home duties into projections of economic dependency ratios.

Composition of Support

Demographic trends affect not only the overall levels of dependency in a population. They also have a bearing on the mix of types of support which comprises the overall package of support provided to dependent segments. There are three main types of support — that provided by the family, the market and the state.[1] Demographic changes can lead to shifts in the division of the support burden between these three channels — between the family and the state, between the family and the market, and between the market and the state.

It is difficult to disentangle the complex ways in which these shifts occur or to arrive at an estimate of their net effect. All we can do is identify some of them and point to their existence. This will leave us short of any clear quantification of their impact but it may help us to avoid some of the distortions which might otherwise occur. We will deal with these issues as they arise later in the report but here we will point to two important areas — the impact of population ageing (i.e. growing numbers of older people and falling numbers of children) and of changing unemployment levels.

The Impact of Population Ageing

It is clear in this context that population ageing is one of the forces which affects the kinds of support provided. The support of children is largely a private responsibility, which is carried both by the market work of parents (which funds money expenditures on children) and by the informal care provided by parents (see

---

[1] The voluntary sector provides another channel of support. Though it is important in a number of areas, it is difficult to quantify and in any event is of a lower order of magnitude than the three areas mentioned. It is beyond the scope of the present report to examine its significance.

above). State provision, though dominant in certain areas (education and health care) is supplementary rather than primary, particularly in that income support for the majority of children (in the form of Child Benefit) provides for only a fraction of the actual financial cost of children (Carney *et al.*, 1994).

Support for the elderly, by contrast, is overwhelmingly a public responsibility. Eighty per cent of the elderly derive their main income from state pensions (75 per cent from old age pensions plus 5 per cent from public servants retirement pensions), and over 70 per cent of the elderly (who are disproportionately heavy consumers of the health services) are covered by medical cards.[2] Family support for older people, which takes the form especially of informal care for frail elderly, accounts for a small part of overall provision for older people.

Because of these differences in the channels of support drawn upon by old people and children, growth in the numbers of old people and declines in the number of children will have a strong effect on the overall structure of support provision. It will lead to a shift in the burden of support away from the family and the market towards the state. In other words, population ageing may have little impact on the overall level of support which is required, but it may sharply increase the share of that support which has to be provided by the state rather than the family. It thus has cost implications for the tax payer.

However, these cost implications are not the whole story since we also have to consider the possibility of counter-balancing *revenue* implications. The revenue implications arise particularly in connection with the decline in the child population. The large child population in the past was one of the factors which kept female labour force participation at relatively low levels in Ireland. As we have seen, mothers' time is one of the main forms of support required by children. A fall in the numbers of children, therefore, will reduce this demand on women's time and will have the effect of releasing large numbers of women for participation in the labour force. This in turn will mean that the numbers paying in-

---

[2] Unpublished data from the ESRI's Survey of the Over-65s in Ireland, 1993. See Fahey and Murray (1994) for further details on this source.

come tax and social insurance contributions will rise and will thus enlarge the support base for the pensions system and other state provisions for older people (this possibility, in fact, has been coming to pass quite strongly in Ireland in the mid-1990s). The combination of fewer children and more old people will thus give rise to a change in the capacity of the support system to deliver resources. This change parallels the change in resources which is required, which means that the degree of imbalance in the support system may well be much less than one would expect.

The Impact of Unemployment

If population ageing is the main demographic force which tends to shift dependence away from the family and the market towards the state, a decline in unemployment would give rise to shifts in the opposite direction. This is so in the first instance because the unemployed themselves would cease to be dependent and as potential payers of income taxes would contribute to the support of those who are dependent. In addition, unemployment among parents means that the market component in family transfers fails. Unemployed parents lack the money incomes from paid work which enable them to finance direct expenditures on children. These have to be replaced by state transfers. To the extent that such transfers are inadequate, poverty for children and their parents is the result.

Future declines in unemployment, therefore, to the extent that it occurred among parents and was not concentrated among the childless (for example, younger people who have not yet started a family), would reduce dependence among children on the state, as well as among the adults directly involved. This reduction would operate through a number of mechanisms:

1. Claims for child dependent allowances among unemployed parents would decline;

2. The incidence of unmarried parenthood might be reduced in that mothers might be more inclined to marry the fathers of their children if those fathers had better employment prospects and thus were likely to be able to play a useful provider role (Hannan and Ó Riain, 1992); and

3. In cases where lone parenthood occurs, absent fathers would be more capable of providing maintenance for their children.

It is not possible to predict how strong any of these individual influences is likely to be, much less what the net effect on the private/public balance of support provision for children is likely to be. Clearly, however, the shifts away from state provision towards provision by the family and the market would be substantial.

Conclusion

This chapter first examined a number of ways in which the support requirements associated with a particular population structure can be defined and measured. All of the approaches considered have in common that they rest on a crude division of the population into dependent and productive segments and a quantification of the ratio between the two segments. Three principal measures of this type were described and assessed — age-dependency ratios, needs weighted age-dependency ratios, and economic dependency ratios. None of these measures are adequate on their own, and even the three combined are affected by the simplistic nature of the underlying dualistic divisions of the population on which they rely. Nevertheless, the measures have some value as indicators of support requirements, particularly where (as in the present instance) the focus is on trends over time rather than levels at any given time.

The second main issue identified in the chapter was the link between population structure and the ways in which support could be channelled from the productive to the dependent segments of the population. The three main channels pointed to were the family, the market and the state. The concern of this discussion was to point out, firstly, that when considering the impact of demographic change on support requirements, compositional shifts in the means by which support could be provided can be as important for policy as changes in the overall level of support which is required, and secondly, that the impact of demographic changes on the composition of support is not simple and linear but is many-sided and contradictory, so that the net outcome is difficult to estimate.

Chapter 3

Trends in Dependency and Support

Introduction

This chapter considers the broad trends in overall support requirements which are associated with actual and projected demographic change. Age-dependency ratios are the simplest and most widely used indicators for this purpose, and we look at those first, both over time and in international comparison. We then consider measures of support ratios which are based on needs-related weights for children and adults. As indicated in Chapter 2, it is far from clear if such weighting of dependency ratios is empirically justified, but we include reference to the resulting measures here for illustrative purposes. Finally, the chapter deals with trends in economic dependency. Under this heading, the division between the dependent and productive segments of the population is based on working status rather than on age and thus gives a somewhat more realistic representation of support requirements than indicators of dependency based on age alone.

The data for the present chapter are drawn mainly from the 1995 CSO population projections, using the low-migration and high-fertility scenario presented in those projections (CSO, 1995). As already noted in Chapter 1, that scenario has so far proven to be the most accurate of those presented in the projections, but it is nevertheless somewhat inaccurate in that it underestimated the rate of population and labour force growth up to 1996. This occurred because it assumed a substantial net outflow of migrants up to 1996, in place of the small net inflow which actually occurred. Since migration occurs mainly among young adults, the lower than expected migration means that the size of the active adult population is likely to be somewhat greater than projected. The positive nature of the dependency trends pointed to in the present chapter, and the positive tone of the whole of the present report, would therefore probably be reinforced by a more up-to-date revision of the projections.

Age Composition and Age-dependency Ratios

Figure 3.1 presents a long-term view of the actual and projected size and age-composition of the population of Ireland by focusing on the period from 1926 to 2026 (see also Appendix Table A.1).

Figure 3.1: Age Composition of Actual and Projected Population, 1926–2026 (millions)

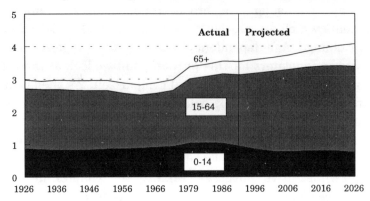

Sources: Actual — CSO data diskettes; Projected — CSO (1995), low-migration, high-fertility assumptions.

Total population contracted slightly between 1926 and 1961, especially in the last decade of that period. The productive age-ranges (those aged 15–64) took the brunt of this contraction, much of which was due to the heavy migration outflow which occurred in the late 1940s and 1950s. A population recovery took place in the 1970s, partly because of a surge in births and partly because of a growth in the numbers in the 15–64 age-group. The latter was fuelled in part by the first and only sustained bout of net inward migration to take place into Ireland since statistical records began. Fertility reached its peak in 1980 and thereafter fell steadily. In consequence, the child population surged in the 1970s but began to decline in numbers from the early 1980s onwards.

The projections of future population included in Figure 3.1 are based on the assumption the total fertility rate (TFR)[1] will show only a small decline from the levels of the 1990s up to 2026 (that is, a fall from 1.93 in 1993 to 1.8 in 2026). If that assumption proves accurate, while total population will grow, the size of the child population will fall during the 1990s but thereafter will remain more or less stable for the first two decades of the next century. The alternative fertility scenario considered by the CSO, which assumes a fall in TFR to 1.5 by 2026, would lead to a considerably smaller child population than that shown in Figure 3.1 (see Chapter 4 for an analysis of fertility trends).

The population aged 15–64 is projected to continue to grow steadily, however, and this growth is projected to continue up to the end of the period we are concerned with (2026). The elderly population shows a stable trend for most of the period examined: it remained at an almost constant share of the total population from 1926 to the present. That share is projected to grow slightly up to about 2010, and thereafter to increase at a somewhat faster rate.

Figure 3.2 (see also Table A.1) converts the absolute numbers shown in Figure 3.1 into age-dependency ratios. Looking at the total age-dependency ratio (those aged under 15 plus those aged 65 and over as a percentage of those aged 15–64), there is a quite pronounced peaking of the trend in the 1960s, and at a very high level. Total dependency reached 73 per cent in the 1960s, having risen from 60 per cent in the 1930s. By 1991, total dependency had fallen back to the level of the 1930s and the CSO's forecasts are that it will continue a steep decline until the middle of the next decade. By 2006, the forecast is that total age dependency will have fallen to the unprecedentedly low level of about 50 per cent. Thereafter it will begin to rise again, but by 2026, it is projected to be at 54 per cent, still well below the levels which prevailed throughout most of the present century. As far as total age-dependency is concerned, therefore, the next thirty years will be far more favourable than the last thirty years.

---

[1] The total fertility rate is the number of children the average woman would have if in the course of her fertile years she experienced the birth rate observed over all age groups in a particular year.

**Figure 3.2: Age-dependency Ratios, 1926–2026
(per 100 aged 15–64)**

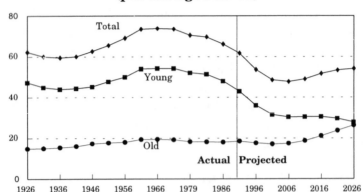

Source: Derived from Figure 3.1

Figure 3.2 also shows that movements in youth dependency are the main contributors to the trend in total dependency over the period 1926–2026. The child population had begun to expand in the 1950s as the active population was contracting, thus sharply altering the balance between them. This movement was reversed in the 1980s: the child population began to contract while the active population expanded, so that young dependency fell well below the previous lows of the 1930s and 1940s. The projections are that the child population will fall even further in the early decades of the next century as the active population continues to expand, thus reducing young dependency to very low levels by Irish standards. It is notable also that in 1981, there were almost three times as many children as old people (just over one million children compared to 368,000 old people). By 2026, the CSO forecast shown in Figure 3.2 is that the numbers of children and old people will converge at around 700,000 each (alternative fertility scenarios considered by the CSO show the child population falling below 600,000 by 2026).

As Figure 3.3 shows, the Irish trend in age-dependency ratios has been distinctive by the standards of other developed countries. Youth dependency was very high from the 1960s to the

Figure 3.3: Age-dependency Ratios, Ireland, UK and all Developed Countries 1960–2025

A. Youth Dependency (per 100 aged 15-64)

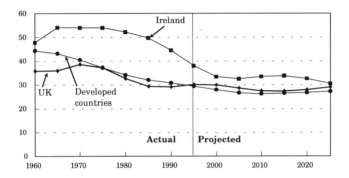

B. Old Dependency (per 100 aged 15-64)

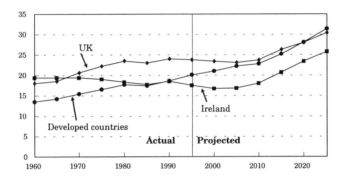

C. Total Dependency (per 100 aged 15-64)

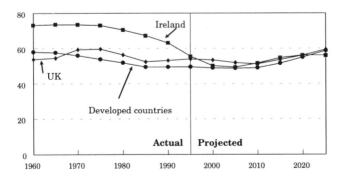

Source: United Nations (1995).

present. It is likely to converge on the international norm in the early decades of the next century, though even then it will be somewhat above the average. Old dependency was also somewhat above the norm in the 1960s but it is now crossing over to a level below the international norm. The net result is that Ireland will move from what, by the standards of developed countries, is a uniquely high age-dependency ratio over recent decades to a quite normal level in the early decades of the next century.

We can see these comparisons in more detail in Figure 3.4, where Ireland's young and old dependency ratios in 1960 (actual) and 2020 (projected) are compared with those of a number of other European countries (the projections used here are those of the United Nations, 1995). In 1960, Ireland had the highest old dependency ratio among the countries listed at 19.4 per cent. By 2020, it is projected to have the lowest, at 23 per cent. The smallness of this increase in the old dependency ratio in Ireland is quite striking compared to the large increases in other countries over the same period (e.g., from 17 to 32 per cent in Germany, from 13 to 30 per cent in Spain). Ireland also had the highest youth dependency in 1960 (54 per cent), and it is likely to have the highest in 2020 also (33 per cent). However, Ireland's outlier status in youth dependency is projected to be much less pronounced in 2020 than in 1960.

These comparisons highlight the paradoxical character of Irish age-dependency ratios in recent decades. In the 1960s, the Irish population, quite oddly, was both very young and very old by the standards of other western countries. This was so because so many of those in the active age ranges had gone missing during the huge emigration wave of the 1950s, leaving substantial populations of children and old people behind. The legacy of that loss is still evident in the smallness of the cohort now in the ages from around 55 to 65. The population recovery since the 1960s is now leading to the opposite paradox — the population is now neither young nor old but increasingly dominated by active adults.

Figure 3.4: Old and Young Dependency in Selected European Countries, 1960 and 2020

A. Old Dependency (elderly per 100 aged 15–64)

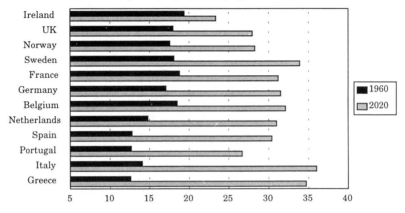

B. Young Dependency (young per 100 aged 15–64)

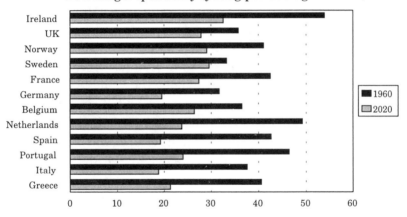

Source: United Nations (1995).

Needs-weighted Age-dependency Ratios

As already noted in Chapter 2, one criticism that might be made of age-dependency ratios as indicators of trends in support requirements is that they take no account of possible differences in the level of support required by different categories of those in the dependent ages. In particular, the standard way of computing age-dependency ratios assumes that the average child aged under 15 requires more or less the same overall level of support as the average elderly person. Changes in the size of the child population are thus taken to have the same significance for support requirements as changes in the size of the elderly population. As an alternative to this standard approach, it has sometimes been argued that elderly people may have higher support requirements than children, so that some weighting of age-dependency ratios is necessary to improve the extent to which they reflect real support requirements. We considered this alternative approach at some length in Chapter 2 and concluded that it probably was not empirically justified. It is based on ways of comparing the costs of children and old people which largely ignore the very large hidden costs of children represented by the time parents expend on looking after them. It has greater validity where the focus is on the financial costs of children and older people, though in that context it is important to remember that financial costs represent only part of the total picture.

Despite the limitations of the measure, it is worth setting out how a needs-weighting of age-dependency ratios along the lines suggested by this alternative approach would affect the picture of past and future support requirements in Ireland which has been set out above. For this purpose, we adopt the weights used as a "first approximation" to calculating needs-weighted support ratios in the works referred to earlier (Cutler *et al.*, 1990; Leibfritz *et al.*, 1995; see p. 16). In those works, a weight of 0.72 was attached to people aged under 20, of 1 to people aged 21–64 and of 1.27 to people aged 65 and over. In the present instance, we take the same weights but utilise a somewhat different division between the young and active age-groups. To maintain consistency with the rest of the present report, we define the young as those aged under 15 rather than those aged under 20. This change in age boundaries makes a certain difference to the levels of dependency indicated by the measure but little difference to the trend over time.

Total age-dependency ratios for the period 1926–2026 which are weighted in this way are compared with the unweighted ratios in Figure 3.5. The comparison shows that the effect of weighting is to flatten out the long-term trend somewhat but not to change its underlying shape. The 1960s still emerge as the peak years for total age-dependency and the first decade of the next century is still projected to provide a long-term low. A resurgence in total age-dependency is still projected to occur in the 2010s but nevertheless emerges at a somewhat lower level in 2026 than in the late 1980s and early 1990s.

Figure 3.5: Total Age-dependecy Ratios, Needs-weighted and Unweighted, 1926–2026

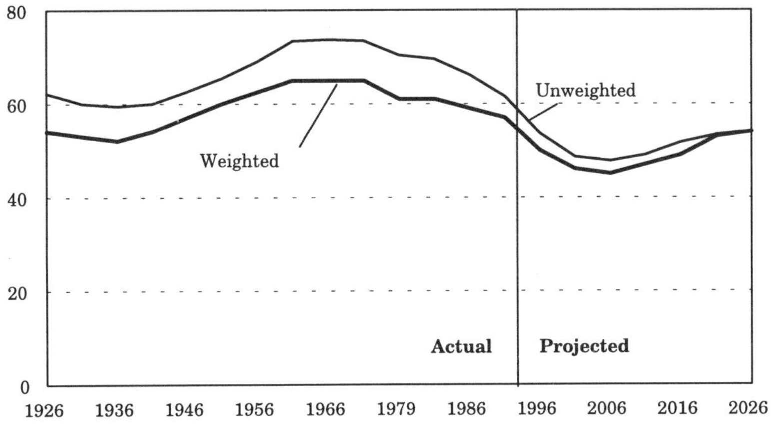

Source: CSO (1995) and text.

This exercise shows that even if we were to accept that the support requirements of older people were a great deal higher than those of children (a proposition which appears doubtful), future dependency ratios in Ireland still seem likely to be a good deal more favourable than those of recent decades.

Economic Dependency

A final issue to be considered in dealing with trends in support requirements is the *economic* dependency ratio, that is, the ratio between the numbers who are economically productive and the rest of the population (see Chapter 2). Here we take the numbers recorded as "at work" as a measure of the economically productive and treat the rest of the population as dependent. As noted in Chapter 2, this approach is misleading in some ways. It treats those engaged in home duties as dependent rather than productive and thus fails to reflect the large element of economic production represented by unpaid housework and childcare. However, since no projections have been made of the numbers engaged in housework, no better alternative is readily available.

Figure 3.6 sets out the trend in this measure for the period 1961–2010 for Ireland, with comparative data for the EU for the years 1971, 1981 and 1991. Because of the large number of factors which affect the size of the labour force, each of which are difficult to predict on their own, the CSO has not made labour force forecasts beyond the year 2006. Even at that, it does not disaggregate the projected labour force into employed and unemployed. Forfás (1996), on the basis of projections prepared by the ESRI, presents summary projections of the labour force, employment and unemployment for the year 2010 and these are used in Figure 3.6 to project the trend in economic dependency out to that year. More recent data show that the assumptions used for both the CSO and the Forfás projections overstate emigration in the first half of the 1990s (see Chapter 1) and may well do so for the remainder of the century as well. Since emigration generally slows down the rate of labour force growth, it is therefore quite possible that they underestimate the rate of labour force growth over the coming years and as a result may understate the degree of downward movement likely to occur in economic dependency over the next ten to fifteen years.

**Figure 3.6: Economic Dependency, 1961–2010
(dependants per 100 workers)**

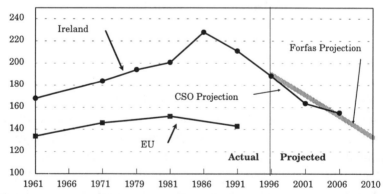

Sources: CSO (1995, assuming 10 percent unemployment rate in 2006);
Forfás, 1996; EUROSTAT, 1993

Figure 3.6 shows that economic dependency in Ireland has been declining sharply since it reached a very high peak in the mid-1980s. It is projected to continue on a downward slope into the next century. The extent of the transformation in economic dependency is dramatic. The number of dependants per 100 workers exceeded 220 in the mid-1980s — a uniquely high level in the EU at the time. It is expected to fall below 160 in 2006 and (according to Forfás projections) to about 133 in 2010.

This positive trend in economic dependency closely reflects the picture from trends in age dependency drawn earlier — the high burdens of the past are now easing and are expected to continue to do so in the years ahead. Trends in economic dependency differ in one respect from the trends in age dependency described earlier in that economic dependency levels peaked in the 1980s while age-dependency levels peaked around the 1960s. This difference arises because the proportion of those in the active age ranges who were at work was higher in the 1960s than in the 1980s, so that economic dependency was lower in the 1960s than the high age-dependency levels might lead one to expect. This in turn was so because unemployment was much lower in the 1960s than in the 1980s, and the participation of young people in paid work was much higher, largely because few young people in the 1960s continued in full-time education beyond their mid-teens. In the 1980s, declining age dependency was more than counterbalanced as far as economic dependency was concerned by a rise in the proportion of those in the active age ranges who were either unemployed or in full-time education.

On the basis of CSO projections, Figure 3.7 decomposes the trend in dependants per 100 workers into its main constituent parts — economic dependency among the young, the old and others. "Others" in this context includes those who are neither young nor old but are not counted as "at work" — the unemployed, those in home duties, those in full-time education, the ill and disabled. All three forms of economic dependency peaked at around the same time in the 1980s, though in the case of old economic dependency, one should really speak of an almost flat long-term trend with only a slight rise in the 1980s. It is important to note that old economic dependency is projected to be *lower* in 2006 than in 1986 (31 elderly per 100 workers in 2006 compared to 35 in 1986). This simply means that the growth in the numbers at work over this period is expected to be greater than the relative growth in the numbers of elderly.

Figure 3.7: Young, Old and Other Economic Dependency, 1961–2006 (per 100 at work)

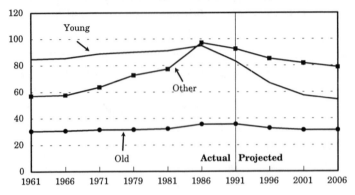

Source: CSO (1995)

Unemployment

The favourable trends in economic dependency just outlined rely partly on a decline in unemployment from the high levels of the late 1980s and early 1990s. The projection for the numbers at work in 2006, on which the dependency estimates in Figure 3.7 are based, assumes an unemployment rate in that year of 10 per cent (see Chapter 5 below for further examination of unemployment trends). By historical standards, an unemployment rate of 10 per cent could be regarded as high, though it is much lower than the peaks of the late 1980s and early 1990s. Unemployment declined from 16.1 per cent in 1992 to 12.6 per cent in 1996 (standardised unemployment rates derived from International Labour Organisation (ILO) measures in the Labour Force Surveys) and is still moving downwards. However, assumptions about the unemployment rate in ten or even five years time are no more than educated guesswork. The ESRI's *Medium Term Review* of 1994 forecast a decline in the unemployment rate from 17 per cent in 1993 to 13.4 per cent in 2000 but current events show that this was excessively cautious. The recent Forfás projections assume that unemployment can be reduced to 6 per cent by 2010, despite labour force growth of 15 per cent over the same period. This assumption seems more plausible now than it did even some months ago, on account of the current strong performance of the Irish economy, but inevitably there must still be a great deal of uncertainty about developments in labour market supply and demand over such a long time-span. In any event, the point to note is that even if unemployment does not fall to such an extent, economic dependency is still likely to decline in the future because of growth in the total labour force and declines in the numbers of certain categories of the non-active, especially children.

Conclusion

The present chapter has looked at trends in a number of measures of dependency in Ireland, both over time and in comparison with the international norm for developed countries. The key conclusion which emerges from this analysis is strong and consistent across each of the measures examined. Ireland has had very high dependency levels both by its own historical standards and by international standards over much of the past three decades. However, these high levels are now on a downward slope, they are expected to continue to decline for about another ten years, and though they may begin to rise again after 2006, they are unlikely to reach anything like the very high levels of recent decades over the next 30 years.

In the case of one of the measures we examined, the economic dependency ratio, present and future decline is as much a matter of economic change (especially change in Ireland's labour market performance) as demographic change. It depends critically on the trend in unemployment, which at present is projected to be steadily downward. This projected decline in unemployment is expected to take place not because of a shrinking supply of labour (in fact the labour supply is expected to increase substantially) but because of greatly increased demand for labour. While the ESRI's *Medium Term Review* of 1994 predicted steady employment growth up to the year 2000, those predictions proved to be too cautious and now need to be revised substantially upwards.

As far as dependency levels are concerned, therefore, Ireland is now on quite a different trajectory from that which is common in many other countries and is causing concern in some of those countries. The principal difference is that Ireland's very high dependency levels are now a thing of the past, and they are unlikely to recur in such a severe form within the foreseeable future. Other western countries experienced much lighter dependency levels in the past than did Ireland. Those countries are now facing the prospect of a long-term steady increase in dependency levels, though it seems unlikely that they will rise to the heights often experienced in Ireland over the last three decades. To oversimplify somewhat, as far as dependency levels are concerned Ireland's past is their future, and their past is Ireland's future. It would be misleading therefore to pay too much attention to emerging dependency trends in other countries as a guide to Ireland's future experience.

Chapter 4

Trends in Fertility and Marriage

Introduction

The decline in fertility has been one of the most important of the demographic changes to occur in Ireland in recent years and, as we have seen in Chapter 3, it is a major contributor to the decline in dependency levels which is now underway in Ireland. The year 1980 recorded the highest total number of births in the country in the present century (at 74,388). By the end of the 1980s, however, the total had fallen to the lowest on record at 51,669 in 1989. Since then it has fallen further to around 48,000 in 1995, representing a decline of more than a third in a decade-and-a-half. For most of the present century, Ireland has had exceptionally high fertility rates by European standards. In the 1960s, the large child population which resulted from high fertility was a major contributor to the exceptionally high age-dependency levels then experienced in Ireland. Today Irish fertility is no longer exceptional, though Ireland belongs among those countries at the upper edge of the range of fertility patterns found in Europe. For the foreseeable future Irish fertility, in common with that of other western countries, seems likely to stabilise below the level which would ensure the natural replacement of the population.

Along with the fall in total fertility Ireland has experienced a rapid growth in the share of fertility occurring outside marriage. In the early 1960s, the share of births taking place outside marriage had fallen to a historic low, at less than 3 per cent. By the early 1990s, almost one-in-five births occurred outside of marriage. More significantly, one-in-three of *first births* (that is, of new family start-ups) occurred outside of marriage in the early 1990s, indicating a sharp decline in marriage as the first phase of new family formation. The significance of this development for our present concerns is not so much that it affects overall dependency levels — children still have to be supported whether they are reared in two-parent rather than one-parent families — but that it signifies a certain increase in the share of the dependency burden for children which is borne by the state (see Chapter 1).

The purpose of the present chapter is to examine these trends in some detail. Data limitations mean that it is not possible to consider many key questions concerning the fertility decline (for example, we have no adequate data on its social class composition), but it is possible to highlight certain important features which have a bearing on the central concerns of the present report.

Falling Fertility

In the 1960s, when the birth rate was falling elsewhere in Europe, it remained fairly stable in Ireland. This pattern continued throughout the 1970s by which time the Irish rate was markedly above the rate in many other countries in Europe. It was only in the 1980s that it declined rapidly (Figure 4.1). However, even with the rapid decline in the birth rate in recent years it was still quite high by European standards in 1994, lying somewhat below the birth rate for Sweden, the highest in the EU, and close to the birth rate for the UK (Figure 4.2). The lowest birth rates in the EU are currently observed in the southern European countries of Spain, Greece, Portugal and Italy.

Figure 4.1: Birth Rate (births per thousand)

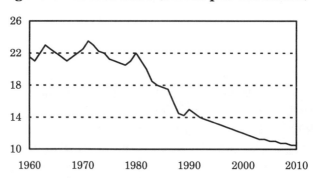

Source: Central Statistics Office: *Vital Statistics*

Figure 4.2: Birth Rate — International Comparisons

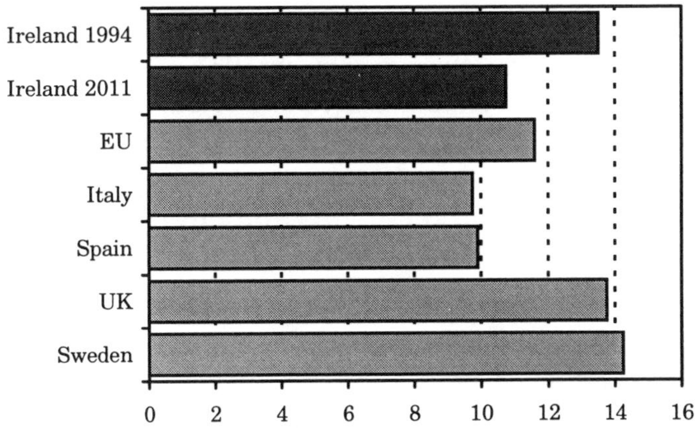

Sources: Council of Europe: Recent Demographic Developments; Central Statistics Office: Vital Statistics

The high birth rate in the 1970s corresponded with a period when the number of women in the child-bearing age groups was rising. If average fertility per woman had remained unchanged this would have led to a continuous rise in the birth rate throughout the 1970s and 1980s. In fact, as Figure 4.1 shows, the birth rate remained more or less unchanged during the 1970s before beginning the steep decline of the 1980s. To understand the factors driving this changing pattern it is important to look behind these numbers.

The Total Fertility Rate (TFR) is an artificial measure of the number of children the average woman of child-bearing age could expect to have if she experienced the birth rate observed over all age groups in a particular year. In practice, average completed family size may prove rather different if, for example, births are temporarily postponed or other factors intervene to produce essentially temporary changes in fertility. However, by definition, completed family size can only be measured when women have passed beyond child-bearing years and the TFR remains an essential measure of current trends in fertility.

Figure 4.3 shows the Total Fertility Rate for Ireland for the period 1961 to 1994. This indicates that, if anything, fertility rose in the 1960s. However, it began to fall around 1970 from a TFR of four per woman to three per woman in 1981. (As already noted, the overall birth rate remained more or less stable between 1971 and 1981, indicating that the fall in TFR in that period was

Figure 4.3: Total Fertility Rate in Ireland

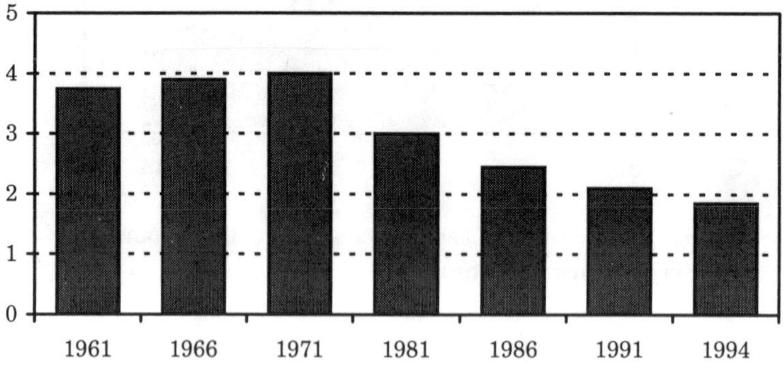

Source: Central Statistics Office: *Vital Statistics*

counter-balanced by a rise in the number of women in the child-bearing ages.) The fall in TFR has continued in recent years, reaching around two children per woman in 1991 and just over 1.8 in 1994. By any standards this fall in TFR has been rapid and it is not clear how much further it will continue. If the pattern observed in the 1970s and 1980s in southern Europe were to be replicated in Ireland this could see an extremely low TFR by early in the next decade. However, it must be observed that fertility in the UK has not shown such an extreme pattern, remaining well above the levels currently observed in Spain, Italy and Greece (Figure 4.4).

Figure 4.4: Completed Family Size (Total Fertility Rates)

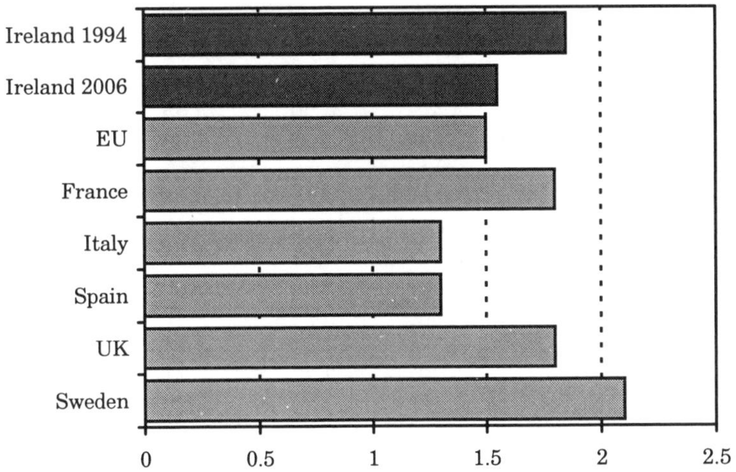

Source: Council of Europe, "Recent Demographic Developments"; ESRI
Forecast

Inter-County Variations in Fertility

Throughout at least the last 30 or 40 years there has been a significant variation in observed levels of fertility within Ireland (for
the late 1970s, see Sexton and Dillon, 1984). Generally, as in the
past, the TFR is lower today in cities than in rural areas. Figure
4.5 shows the TFRs for a sample of three urban counties and
three predominantly rural counties for 1981 and 1991. Full details are given in Table 4.1.

In 1961 the highest fertility was in Tipperary South Riding
and the lowest was in Dublin city. However, fertility was above
average in both Limerick city and Cork city. This remained true
up to 1971 when the TFR was actually higher than in 1961. Between 1971 and 1981 a major change occurred with the TFR for
the country dropping by over 0.9 children. The fall was substantially higher in Dublin city, Dun Laoghaire and Cork city with, on
average, a below-average fall in more rural counties.

Between 1981 and 1991 there was another fall in the TFR of
on average just over 1. However, in this case the drop in Dublin
and Cork cities was below the national average and a more rapid

Welfare Implications of Demographic Trends

Table 4.1: Total Fertility Rate by County, 1961–91

	1961	1971	1981	1991
Ireland	**3.76**	**3.96**	**3.04**	**2.08**
Leinster	**3.69**	**3.85**	**2.90**	**1.99**
Carlow	4.40	4.90	3.68	2.35
Dublin County Borough	3.39	3.50	2.34	1.60
Dublin Belgard	NA	NA	NA	2.15
Dublin Fingal	NA	NA	NA	2.19
Dun Laoghaire-Rathdown	NA	NA	NA	1.73
Dun Laoghaire	3.45	4.05	2.65	NA
Dublin County (old)	3.74	3.58	2.85	NA
Dublin County	3.66	3.65	2.82	2.01
Kildare	4.35	4.76	3.44	2.26
Kilkenny	3.79	4.17	3.11	2.29
Laois	4.16	4.13	3.28	2.18
Longford	3.92	4.57	3.60	2.62
Louth	3.79	4.12	3.22	2.04
Meath	3.82	4.32	3.46	2.20
Offaly	4.35	4.34	3.30	2.29
Westmeath	4.29	4.32	3.59	2.24
Wexford	4.10	4.33	3.60	2.37
Wicklow	3.79	4.16	3.24	2.31
Munster	**3.87**	**4.05**	**3.16**	**2.14**
Clare	3.83	4.21	3.27	2.31
Cork County Borough	3.94	4.08	2.58	1.83
Cork County	3.61	3.93	3.30	2.13
Kerry	3.72	3.77	3.24	2.15
Limerick County Borough	4.06	4.43	2.85	2.16
Limerick County	4.14	4.05	3.29	2.29
Tipperary N.	4.01	4.23	3.68	2.41
Tipperary S.	4.52	4.20	3.31	2.15
Waterford County Borough	3.75	3.87	2.61	1.82
Waterford County	3.72	3.89	3.31	2.35
Connacht	**3.76**	**4.22**	**3.26**	**2.25**
Galway County Borough	NA	NA	NA	1.68
Galway County	NA	NA	NA	2.52
Galway (Total)	3.87	4.47	3.13	2.19
Leitrim	3.70	4.27	3.69	2.34
Mayo	3.77	4.14	3.49	2.40
Roscommon	3.59	3.69	3.23	2.25
Sligo	3.69	4.08	3.06	2.15
Ulster (part of)	**3.70**	**4.03**	**3.47**	**2.37**
Cavan	4.01	4.17	3.75	2.63
Donegal	3.49	4.02	3.49	2.38
Monaghan	3.79	3.90	3.17	2.09

Source: Census of Population and Vital Statistics.

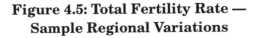

**Figure 4.5: Total Fertility Rate —
Sample Regional Variations**

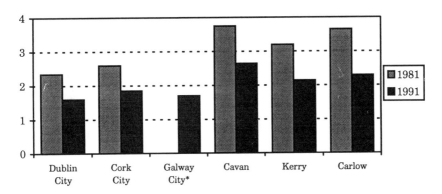

* Data for 1981 not available
Source: Table 4.1

drop occurred in rural counties. The drop was higher in the three
Ulster counties than in the other three provinces, reflecting their
totally rural character. This still left a fairly significant difference
in fertility between the urban and rural areas of the country in
1991 with the TFR being under 2 in Dublin city, Dun Laoghaire-
Rathdown, Cork city, Waterford city and Galway city. All other
counties displayed a TFR of over 2. However, the gap between the
highest and the lowest counties was significantly smaller than at
any time since 1961.

Non-Marital Births

As shown in Figure 4.6, the last 30 years have also seen a major
growth in the proportion of all births which are accounted for by
single mothers. Between 1961 and 1981 there was a slow rise
from under 2 per cent of births occurring to single mothers to just
over 5 per cent in 1981. However, since 1981 the situation has
changed radically so that by 1994, 20 per cent of all births occurred to single mothers.

Figure 4.7 and Table 4.2 show the rise in fertility of single
women since 1971 by age of mother. Between 1971 and 1981 the
biggest change occurred in the birth rate for single women between 20 and 24 with significant changes for the other cohorts

Figure 4.6: Births to Single Mothers, 1961–1994
(% of all births)

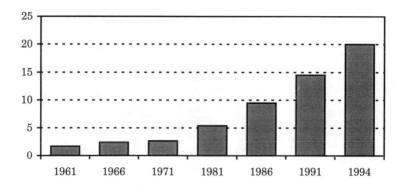

Source: Central Statistics Office: *Vital Statistics*

under 30. However, since 1981 it is very striking how the birth rate for single mothers has changed to the extent that it is over 20 per thousand for single women in their 30s — very similar to the rate observed for single women in their 20s. The increase in the birth rate for single women between 1981 and 1991 was below average for women under 20.

Figure 4.7: Birth Rate of Single Women (by Age Group, births per thousand)

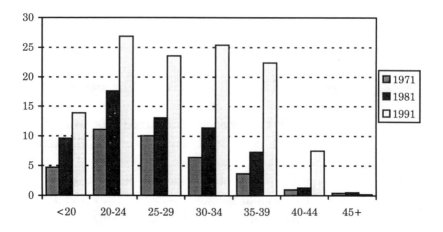

Source: Central Statistics Office: *Vital Statistics*

Table 4.2: Births per 1000 Single Women

Age	1961	1966	1971	1981	1986	1991
<20	2.7	3.4	4.7	9.6	11.4	13.9
20–24	5.3	8.3	11.1	17.6	21.8	26.9
25–29	5.2	8.6	10.1	13.1	19.2	23.6
30–34	4.1	6.2	6.4	11.4	20.4	25.4
35–39	2.0	3.1	3.7	7.3	16.5	22.4
40–44	0.7	1.0	1.0	1.3	3.8	7.5

Source: Census of Population and Vital Statistics

In examining these data on non-marital fertility, two distorting influences on the data should be kept in mind. First, in the past social stigma caused many pregnant single women to move to the UK to have their children. There was probably also a tendency for single mothers from rural areas to move to cities before the birth of their child. The extent by which this tendency for single mothers to migrate on pregnancy has been reduced in recent years will show up as an increase both in the national fertility rates of single women and in the rural rates in particular.

The second factor which must be taken into account is the rise over the last 20 years in the recorded number of women from the Republic choosing to go to the UK to have an abortion. By the early 1990s the number of abortions in the UK registered as being performed on women from Ireland was around 4,000, or around 8 per cent of all births.

An additional significant issue as far as dependency patterns are concerned is the number of births to young single women, particularly those under the age of 20. It is likely that these women and their children will require significant public assistance to overcome their limited command over financial resources, not to speak of other social disadvantages they may experience. Figure 4.8 shows the birth rate for single mothers aged under 20 in certain urban and rural areas. The rate is generally higher in urban than in rural counties in Ireland. However, even within these groups there is considerable variation. For Dublin city the rate is relatively very high, as it is for Limerick and Waterford cities, while it is noticeably lower for Cork city and Galway city.

**Figure 4.8: Birth Rate of Young Single Mothers —
(Sample of Regional Variation)**

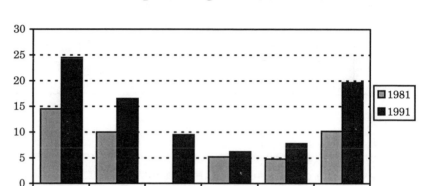

* Data for 1981 not available

Source: Central Statistics Office: *Vital Statistics*

Similarly the rate is high for Carlow and low for Kerry and Cavan. While these data may be distorted by a continuing tendency for some young single mothers to move to cities prior to their child's birth, the regional and class differences in behaviour which these data suggest warrant further research.

At the same time as the fertility of single women has been rising the fertility of married women has shown a very rapid fall. Since 1971 the fall has been greatest for women over the age of 40. However, there was also a major reduction in the observed birth rate for women in their 20s and 30s (Figure 4.9).

As shown in Figure 4.10, by 1994 over 90 per cent of all births to teenagers were to single women and over half of all births to women aged between 20 and 25 were also to single women. However, even with the rise in fertility of single women aged over 25, because the bulk of women in their 30s are married, over 90 per cent of all births to women in these age groups occur to married women.

Figure 4.9: Birth Rate of Married Women (births per thousand married women)

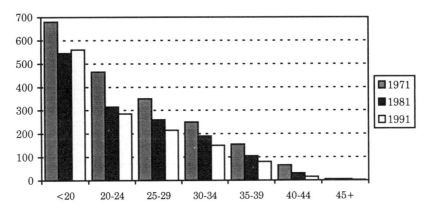

Source: Central Statistics Office: *Vital Statistics*

Figure 4.10: Births to Single Mothers (as a Percentage of All Births by Age of Mother)

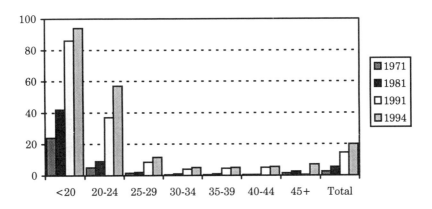

Source: Central Statistics Office: *Vital Statistics*

In interpreting the significance of these data, in particular their implications for state services, it is important to emphasise that the data for single women make no distinction between single women who are involved in a stable relationship and those who do not have the support of the father.

We also have, as yet, little information on whether single mothers remain single indefinitely or whether they subsequently marry or form a long-term relationship. This information could be of considerable importance in determining the implications for state services in the future and it warrants further research. We do know that the trend in lone parenthood is sharply upward and that non-marital parenthood (rather than marital breakdown) is the main driving force in that trend. However, it may well be the case that the number will stabilise as a high proportion of these women eventually marry. From the point of view of public policy it is at least as important to know something about the class and educational attainments of these mothers as to know what will happen to their total numbers. This is an issue for further research.

Trends in Marriage

Over the last 30 years trends in the incidence and age of marriage have been important in influencing the developing pattern of fertility in Ireland. In Figure 4.11 we show the marriage rate since 1970. Traditionally Ireland had a very low marriage rate and where people got married this happened at a relatively late age. This was a vital factor in controlling fertility and the birth rate since the Famine (Walsh 1968). However, in the 1960s the marriage rate increased rapidly. Increasing proportions of successive cohorts of the population married and the mean age at marriage fell for both males and females. The marriage rate peaked in the early 1970s and it has fallen quite rapidly since then, especially since 1981.

Figure 4.12 shows the proportion of women married at different ages in 1994 classified by the level of education completed. This shows that the proportion of the older age groups (over 60) ever married is lower than for the 40 to 60 age group. This reflects the low marriage rate for those of "marriageable age" up to the 1960s. It is interesting that the lower incidence of marriage is particularly pronounced for those older women who have third level education. This may reflect the particularly difficult choice which faced highly educated women in the pre-1970 era. They had to choose between pursuing a career in full-time employment

Figure 4.11: Marriage Rate (Marriages per thousand population)

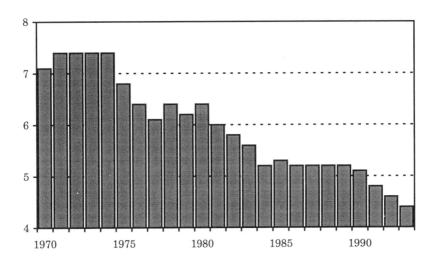

Source: Central Statistics Office: *Vital Statistics*

Figure 4.12: Proportion of Females Ever Married (by Education, 1994, %)

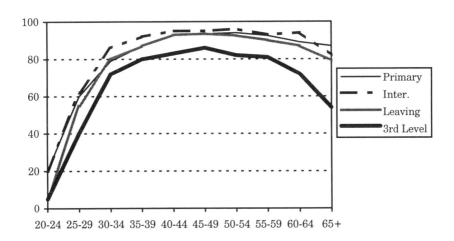

Source: Labour Force Survey

or marrying and having children. The gap between the proportion of women with higher education who are married and the proportion of all other women who are married is somewhat smaller for the 30 to 60 age group but it is, nonetheless, significant, reflecting a continuing tension for such women.[1]

Not surprisingly for women in their 20s the pursuit of higher education tends to rule out early marriage and this is reflected in a substantially lower proportion of such women being married. As shown in Figure 4.13 this is also true for men with third-level education. For men in the older age groups the position is rather different. In Ireland in earlier decades men certainly did not face a choice between having a career and marrying. Instead it would appear to be men with only primary education who had the lowest incidence of marriage (see Figure 4.13). This may reflect differing patterns of behaviour among the rural (predominantly farming) population, compared to the urban population in earlier decades. The tradition that marriage could only be undertaken where the husband had inherited or had the prospect of inheriting the farm may have been a further factor affecting the incidence of marriage among older men in rural areas.

As shown in Figure 4.14 and Table 4.3, even with the recent decline in the marriage rate for those in their 20s, the rate today for those aged 25–29 is not very different from that in 1961. For older age groups there is now a significantly greater proportion of women married than was the case 30 years ago. While the data in Table 4.3 may help explain the fall in the marriage rate, they cannot tell us whether we are observing a major decline in the proportion of the population who will ever be married or, alternatively, a continuing pattern of postponing marriage until women are in their 30s.

---

[1] An alternative explanation is that couples are more compatible when the male is better educated. However, a more plausible explanation is that well-educated women in Ireland in the past would have had greater problems in combining a career with marriage and children.

Figure 4.13: Proportion of Males Ever Married
(by Education, 1994, %)

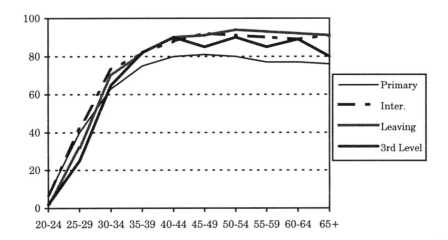

Source: Labour Force Survey

Figure 4.14: Proportion of Women Ever Married
(by Age, %)

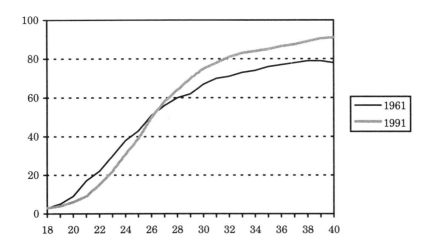

Source: Census of Population

Table 4.3: Proportion of Women Married by Age, %

	1961	1966	1971	1981	1986	1991	1994
15–19	1.11	1.60	2.12	2.33	0.94	0.43	0.22
20–24	21.79	25.22	31.10	32.32	22.34	13.79	8.44
25–29	54.89	62.25	68.85	71.23	64.78	56.65	51.72
30–34	70.39	75.86	80.57	85.39	83.03	79.95	78.35
35–39	76.49	78.75	82.91	88.85	88.75	87.19	86.24
40–44	78.03	80.48	82.20	88.23	89.93	89.90	90.12
45–49	77.94	79.55	81.84	86.62	88.80	90.31	91.43
50–54	75.82	78.91	80.47	84.27	86.83	89.09	91.22
55–59	74.79	76.23	79.35	82.75	84.42	86.99	89.38
60–64	75.16	74.89	76.36	80.88	82.57	84.62	87.15

Source: Census of Population

Education and Marriage

The effects of the changing educational composition of the population on the marriage rate is examined in Table 4.4. Column 1 shows the proportion of women married in each age group in 1981 and the third column gives the same information for 1994. In the middle column we take the proportion of women with primary education in 1981 and multiply this by the proportion of women with primary education who were married in 1994; we do the same for women at each of the four standards of education and sum the result. When one makes this adjustment, the change in the proportion of women married under 30 between columns 1 and 2 shows the effects of the decline in the proportion of women married independent of education. The smaller difference between columns 2 and 3 shows the effects of the change in the educational attainment of the female population. This shows that if the much higher educational status of the population in 1994 had been observed in 1981, then the later age at marriage common among those with higher levels of education would have had a minor, though significant, impact on the proportion of the population married under 30.

The approach in Table 4.4 assumes that it is the decision of women to marry which is crucial to whether a marriage actually takes place. Obviously there are two parties to a marriage and economic and demographic factors will also have affected men's behaviour. The rise in educational attainment of women was paralleled by that of men over the period, contributing to the trend towards later marriage. It is quite possible that some of the decline in the marriage rate, in particular when educational status is controlled for, was also due to rising male unemployment in the 1980s.

Table 4.4: Effects of Changing Education on Marriage Rate, 1981

Age of woman	1981 actual	1981 at 1994 education-specific marriage rates	1994 actual
20–24	32.3	10.3	8.4
25–29	71.2	55.0	51.7
30–34	85.4	78.8	78.4
35–39	88.8	86.6	86.2
40–44	88.2	90.4	90.1
45–49	86.6	91.6	91.4

Source: Labour Force Survey

The review of the trends in marriage highlight the fact that while in the past this was a vital factor in explaining trends in fertility, the link between marriage and the decision to have children is now much weaker. It is probable that they are both affected by changes in the role of women in society with a far greater participation in the labour force by women of all ages. This change in participation is, itself, partly driven by the change in the educational attainment of the population. Unfortunately data are not currently available which would allow us to examine the pattern of fertility by the social class or educational attainment of the mother. Such data could help throw light on the underlying causes of the rapidly changing pattern of behaviour in the field of marriage and fertility.

The changes which we are observing are probably driven by many different factors which are interacting to produce the changing roles of women and men in society. Changing expectations as a result of increased education as well as wider cultural change are clearly important. The opening up of the economy can have an indirect effect. For example Figure 4.15 shows the proportion of women who have lived abroad for at least a year. (The

Figure 4.15: Females who have resided abroad (1991, by education and age, % of population)

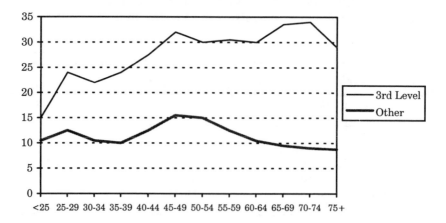

Source: Census of Population

Figure 4.16: Educational Attainment, Females (by year of birth, % of total living in Ireland)

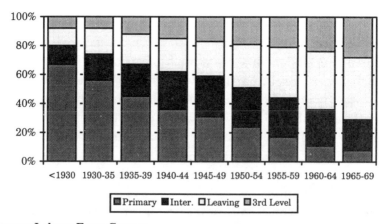

Source: Labour Force Survey

figures for males are similar.) There can be no other country in the EU where at least 10 per cent of its adult population have at some time in the past lived abroad and where between 25 per cent and 30 per cent of its population with third-level education, have had such exposure to life in another culture or society.

Underlying these changes is the tremendous change in the educational composition of the population. Figure 4.16 shows the educational profile of the adult female population in Ireland in 1994 (the profile for men is generally similar, though the male educational levels are slightly lower in general than female levels) and thus reflects the proportions leaving school with different educational levels over the last 50 years. Where the bulk of the older population has a minimal level of education, changes since the 1960s have meant that third-level education is the norm for between a third and a half of younger adults and completed second-level education is the norm for around three-quarters of younger adults.

Low Fertility and Population Replacement

It is worth considering briefly the implications of below-replacement fertility for Ireland's demographic future, since it seems likely that fertility at that low level is likely to continue in Ireland for some years. In many western countries, the arrival of below-replacement fertility has raised the prospect of zero growth or even a long-term decline in population, a prospect which is quite novel for those countries and has given rise to the unease which is often caused by the unfamiliar. As with so many other things, Ireland is different in this regard, not so much in that a zero-growth or declining population is unlikely to emerge here as that such an experience would be nothing new to modern Irish demographic history. The paradox is that while Irish fertility was far above population replacement levels for most of the present century, and indeed was the highest in the western world for much of this period, Ireland still had the poorest record in population replacement — it was the only western country to sustain long-term decline in population since the latter half of the nineteenth century. To add to the paradox, it is only with the much lower fertility rates of recent decades that population replacement has begun to take place.

The resolution to these paradoxes, of course, is that migration has been as big a force in modern Irish population history as fertility. For most of the present century, though birth cohorts have been large, survivorship in Ireland to the prime adult ages has been extraordinarily poor, principally because of the devastating effect of emigration (infant and early adulthood mortality played a much lesser role).

Figure 4.17 illustrates the actual record of population replacement in Ireland since early in this century and the projected performance for early in the next by showing the survivorship in Ireland to age 30–34 of successive birth cohorts (survivorship in this context means not just that persons are alive but that they are living in Ireland). In 1926, for example, the cohort of 30–34 year olds then living in Ireland represented less than half of their birth cohort (those born between 1892–96). For most of the present century, in fact, five-year birth cohorts have exceeded 300,000 (or 60,000 births per year). It was only in the 1970s, however, tłat survivorship rates in Ireland were high enough to raise the cohort of 30–34 years olds above the 200,000 mark (or 40,000 per single year of age). In other words, up to the 1970s, survivorship in Ireland to age 30–34 was never above two-thirds, and was often as low as a half.

**Figure 4.17: Survivorship of birth cohorts
to age 30–34, 1926–2020**

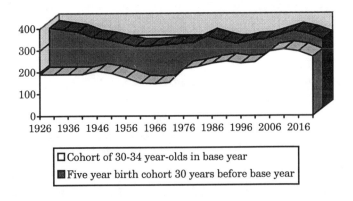

Source: Central Statistics Office: *Census of Ireland*

In the first decade of the next century, the 30–34 year old cohort is projected to break through the 250,000 barrier (50,000 per single year of age). This is due largely to the large size of the birth cohort of the early 1980s, though there is some small gain from improved survivorship in Ireland as well. It is significant that, according to these projections, survivorship to age 30–34 in Ireland will by then have risen to 95 per cent. In the light of more up-to-date information from the 1996 Census of Population, which shows that net emigration disappeared in the period 1991–96, this projection may understate the eventual size of the 30–34 year old cohort (see pp. 8–9). In any event, population performance in the years ahead is likely to be vastly improved by comparison with much of modern Irish demographic history, though it is quite unremarkable by the standards of other countries (in many western countries, survivorship as measured in this way often exceeds 100 per cent, as birth cohorts are added to by substantial in-migration).

It is in this context that we should evaluate the significance of the recent fall in the birth rate in Ireland as far as population replacement is concerned. Since the 1980s, the annual total of births has fallen below 50,000 per year for the first time on record and could fall to 45,000 in the coming decades. However, even with an annual birth rate of 45,000 in the future, population reproduction could be more effective than it has been for most of the present century. If Ireland can hold on to all of those who are born, such a birth rate would yield an eventual cohort aged 30–34 which would be considerably larger than the corresponding cohorts of earlier decades. Such a pattern of population replacement, in fact, would not only be more effective in pure demographic terms than that which has prevailed so often in Ireland. It might also be socially and economically more efficient, on the basis that it is more efficient to produce fewer children and retain them up to and through adulthood in Ireland than to produce large numbers of children but disperse many of them abroad once they pass out of childhood.

Conclusion

The sharp downward movement in fertility has been one of the most important developments in Irish population patterns in recent years, yet it has been little researched and is little understood. We have seen in Chapter 3 that this development has contributed enormously to the decline in dependency levels which has occurred in Ireland in recent years. Fertility is likely to remain low for the future, if not decline further, and so is likely to contribute to a continued downward movement in dependency levels.

In this chapter, we have explored some aspects of fertility trends since the 1960s without attempting a complete analysis, which would be beyond the scope of this book. The available data suggest that falling fertility is closely linked to two other developments — rising levels of education in the population and a decline in the marriage rate. Much of the decline in fertility is due to a retreat from marriage among women of child-bearing age, though it is also due in part to a fall in fertility within marriage. Some of the decline in the marriage rate in turn appears to be linked to the rising educational attainments of women.

The analysis also indicates that women aged under 25 behave differently regarding fertility than do women aged over 25. For the former group, the bulk of child-bearing takes place outside of marriage, whereas for the latter group, child-bearing is still largely confined within marriage. For older women, therefore, the retreat from marriage means a corresponding reduction in child-bearing, whereas for younger women, the effect on fertility of lower marriage rates has been counter-balanced to some extent by a near-parallel growth in non-marital fertility. We have not been able to examine this aspect of present-day fertility behaviour in any detail here, though other studies have pointed to a strong link between child-bearing among young women (whether inside or outside of marriage) and early school-leaving, both among the young fathers involved as well as among the young mothers (see, e.g., Hannan and Ó Riain, 1993). We should also remember that, even for younger women, overall fertility has declined somewhat since the peak of the early 1980s. We should also be careful not to exaggerate the significance of child-bearing in younger women's lives, since the vast majority of younger women do not have children, either inside or outside of marriage.

Chapter 5

Labour Force Participation

Introduction

In Chapter 4, we dealt with the principal force behind the present downward movement in the size of the dependent population in Ireland, the decline in fertility. Here we turn to one of the main forces behind the present upward movement in the size of the productive population, the rise in participation in the labour force, especially among women. Changes in women's labour force participation are closely linked with the changes which are also occurring in fertility and marriage. Underlying them all are wider cultural and economic changes, an important aspect of which is the change in the educational attainment levels of the population.

Compared to the extent of change in female participation in the labour force over the past 25 years, the changes in male participation have been limited. In addition, while the labour force has increased over the long term, employment growth stagnated in the 1980s. The result was a substantial rise in unemployment which, as we saw in Chapter 3, greatly increased the support burden faced by those at work in the 1980s.

In this chapter we first consider recent trends in female labour force participation and some of the factors affecting those trends. We then briefly consider the changes which have occurred in participation by males. We then consider developments in unemployment, and finally offer some observations on possible future developments in labour force patterns.

Female Labour Force Participation

Participation by married women in the labour force as measured in conventional statistics in Ireland has traditionally been very low by European standards but has risen steadily in recent years. Questions have been raised about the meaning and accuracy of

conventional statistics on this issue, especially as long-term series. There are indications that those statistics exaggerate the
increase which has occurred in married women's labour force
participation since the 1960s, principally because they seriously
understate the level of such participation in the earlier part of
that period (Fahey, 1990; 1992). However, though some questions
about the data remain (Fahey, 1992), the accuracy of the statistics
is likely to have improved in the last decade at least, partly because a form of female employment that was particularly difficult
to measure in the past — unpaid labour on family farms — has
declined in importance and partly because new ILO-type approaches have improved both the conceptual and methodological
bases of the data. The present chapter mainly utilises ILO-type
data on women's employment from 1988 onwards, thereby avoid-
ing the more uncertain data from earlier periods.

Future refinements of trend data in this area will need to take
account of the growing incidence of part-time work among women,
perhaps by estimating the number of full-time equivalent jobs
held by women as well as counting the number of women in jobs.
By failing to allow for the part-time nature of much of women's
work, the standard measures of labour force participation tend to
overstate somewhat the recent growth in the labour force.[1] On the
other hand, however, as we note elsewhere (p. 21), participation
by married women even in part-time jobs may have a disproportionately large effect on tax revenues. From a support point of
view, therefore, women's part-time jobs may have a greater significance than the labour-time they involve would suggest.

Even though participation rates for married women in the past
may have been under-measured, they were nevertheless lower
than participation rates for single women and for men. As a result, we first consider the recent trends in the pattern of participation by married women. Figure 5.1 compares the participation
rate by age for all women in 1988 and 1994. This makes clear that

---

[1] In 1995, almost 8 per cent of those in work were in part-time jobs. Taking
women alone, this rises to almost 23 per cent (*Labour Force Survey* 1995,
Tables 28 and 29).

**Figure 5.1: Female Labour Force Participation
(by Age, % of Cohort)**

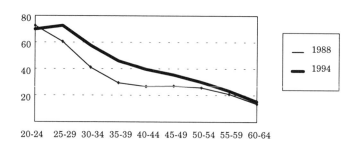

Source: Labour Force Survey

**Figure 5.2: Female Labour Force Participation
(Married Women, %)**

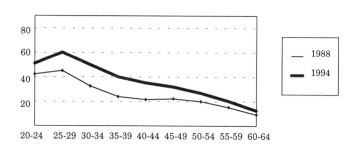

Source: Labour Force Survey

the change has occurred primarily among women aged between 25 and 50. In Figure 5.2 we show the participation rate for married women alone. Because married women constitute the bulk of women over 30 it is not surprising that there is considerable similarity in the two figures reflecting the fact that the rise in female participation is fully attributable to a changed pattern of behaviour among married women.

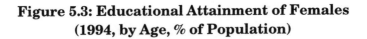

**Figure 5.3: Educational Attainment of Females
(1994, by Age, % of Population)**

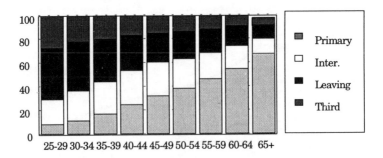

Source: Labour Force Survey

Underlying the change in behaviour has been the change in the educational composition of the population and of the female population in particular.[2] As shown in Figure 5.3, the bulk of women in the older age groups had only primary or limited secondary education. However, among those in their late 20s today, the vast majority have at least completed secondary education and for the cohort leaving school this year the proportion entering third-level education may be as high as 50 per cent.

It has been established for Ireland that the private[3] return to education has been high (Callan, 1993). As a result, as women's educational attainment has risen so too have their potential financial gains from participating in the labour force. In addition, higher levels of education may have helped produce a cultural change where women are more disposed to remaining in the labour force, or to returning to it as their children grow older.

Figures 5.4 to 5.6 show labour force participation for married women classified by highest level of education attained. Labour force participation by those with only primary education is very low (Figure 5.4) and has shown relatively little change since 1988.

---

[2] Generally the female population has a slightly higher level of educational attainment than the male population.

[3] The return to the individual rather than the social rate of return. It does not take account of the wider costs and benefits to society.

The biggest change has occurred in participation rates for married women with education to Leaving Certificate level. The increase in participation rates is especially high (20 percentage points) for those in their 30s and 40s. It is clear that a significant number of women in this category who had dropped out of work at an earlier stage in their career returned to the labour force between 1988 and 1994.

For women with third-level education the participation rate was already high in 1988. For married women under the age of 40 in this category, 60 per cent were already in the labour force in 1988. The biggest change has occurred among women with higher education in their early 40s. Between 1988 and 1994 the participation rate for this group rose by around 20 percentage points indicating that a significant number of such women, who had been out of the labour force in 1988, had returned to it by 1994.

The compound effects of differences in participation rates by education combined with the increase in the average educational attainment of the female population accounts for a certain portion of the rise in female participation. However, there remains a significant growth in participation which is not accounted for by educational change, especially for those women who have completed second-level education. Table 5.1 shows a decomposition of the growth in participation into a change due to the growth in educational attainment and a change due to other exogenous forces. The major decline in participation in the 15–25 age group shown in the table is due to the increase in the numbers of young people remaining on in full-time education, an increase which is also observed for males in the same age group. The table shows that rising educational attainment in the 25–40 age group has had a substantial effect on participation rates but this still leaves the bulk of the change observed over the 1981–94 period to be explained by other factors. Walsh (1993) has studied the issue of female labour force participation in more detail and he shows how a range of other factors, including the economic environment, have contributed to the change in participation rates since 1971.

Figure 5.4: Female Labour Force Participation (Married Women with only Primary Education, %)

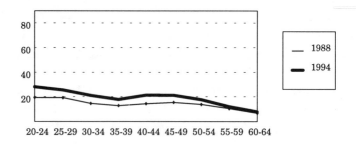

Source: Labour Force Survey

Figure 5.5: Female Labour Force Participation (Married Women with Leaving Cert. Education, %)

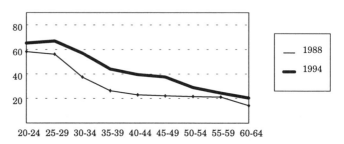

Source: Labour Force Survey

Figure 5.6: Female Labour Force Participation (Married Women with Third-Level Education, %)

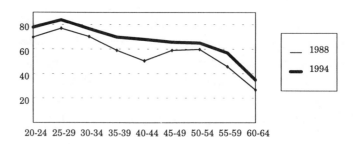

Source: Labour Force Survey

**Table 5.1: Contribution of Education to Rise in
Labour Force Participation 1981–1994**

| Age | *Change between 1981 and 1994 because of:* | | | *1994* |
	Educational Attainment	Other	Total	Actual Participation
15–19	1.0	-69.0	-68.1	15.2
20–24	7.7	-12.5	-4.7	69.7
25–29	11.3	15.7	27.0	72.6
30–34	9.1	21.7	30.8	57.7
35–39	7.2	15.7	22.9	45.9
40–44	6.5	8.8	15.3	39.5
45–49	6.2	4.8	10.9	35.3

Source: Labour Force Survey

In the past marriage played an important part in determining female participation — participation rates were much higher for single women than for married women. Among women aged 25–35 in 1981, for example, a higher proportion of single women than of married women were in the labour force, irrespective of the presence of children (Figure 5.7). It is especially notable that, in 1981, single women *with* children were more likely to be in the labour force than married women *without* children (80 per cent of the former were in the labour force in 1981 compared to less than 70 per cent of the latter).[4] However, between 1981 and the early 1990s, this pattern changed radically in that the presence of children rather than marriage became the crucial factor affecting participation. As shown in Figure 5.7, by 1992 the participation rates for those without children, whether married or single, became almost identical, while the participation rate for single women with children (30 per cent) had fallen slightly below that of married women with children (40 per cent). In other words, mothers had much lower participation rates than women who had no children, irrespective of marital status.

---

[4] The bar on married women working in the civil service was not abolished until 1973.

Figure 5.7: Female Labour Force Participation
(Aged 25–34, %)

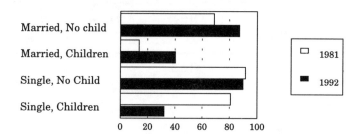

Source: Census 1981 and Labour Force Survey 1992

The change in behaviour among single mothers since the early 1980s probably reflects the growing importance of social welfare payments to lone parents over the period. McCashin (1993, 1996) indicates that social security provisions for lone parents are built on the assumption that they will not be in the labour market, an assumption which he argues has become something of a self-fulfilling prophecy because of the incentive structure it creates. However, we do not know if the educational and class background of lone parents has changed over time and would help explain the change in behaviour. In 1981 of the 8,000 lone parents aged 25–34 approximately a third had only primary education or their level of education was unknown and 10 per cent had third-level education[5]; the remainder (57 per cent) had some form of second-level education. Unfortunately we do not have a similar breakdown for the 1990s.

The participation rate for all single women is shown in Figure 5.8. Between 1988 and 1994 there was very little change in participation among this group of women over the full age-range from

---

[5] It should be stressed that the data in the 1981 census do not readily lend themselves to this analysis and some uncertainty must surround the allocation of women to different categories. In addition, the data on educational attainment are based on somewhat different definitions to those used in the Census and the Labour Force Survey today.

Figure 5.8: Female Labour Force Participation
(Single Women, %)

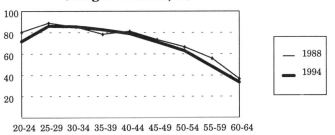

Source: Labour Force Survey

20 to 65. There was a small reduction in the rate for those in the youngest and oldest age groups but, compared to the changes over that period for married women, the differences were small.

However, in Figure 5.9 we show the participation rate for single women with only primary education. As with their married colleagues, there is a big difference in participation rates for single women with limited education compared to the whole

Figure 5.9: Female Labour Force Participation (Single Women with only Primary Education, %)

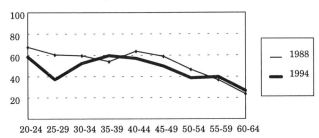

Source: Labour Force Survey

population of single women. There are two possible reasons for this divergence: women with only primary education may have limited earning potential and limited incentive to enter the labour force, and a higher proportion of such women may be single mothers. On balance, the second explanation, higher fertility, seems more likely as low earning potential should not discourage women from entering the labour force, if only to receive their social welfare entitlements.

Male Labour Force Participation

For males there has been a slow reduction in the participation rate below the age of 25, primarily because of rising participation in education. There is also a long-term decline in the participation rate of males aged 55 and over. This decline can be observed among males across all levels of educational attainment, though it is most marked for males with only a primary education (Figures 5.10 to 5.13). The trend towards earlier retirement can be observed in other European countries. In the case of Ireland an additional factor contributing to this trend is the declining importance of agriculture; traditionally farmers who are owner occupiers have continued active on their farms later than would be the case for employees working in other sectors of the economy.

Figure 5.10: Male Labour Force Participation (by Age, %)

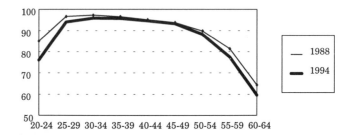

Source: Labour Force Survey

**Figure 5.11: Male Labour Force Participation
(by Completed Education — Primary, %)**

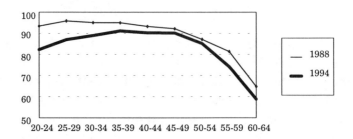

Source: Labour Force Survey

Figure 5.12: Male Labour Force Participation (by Completed Education — Leaving Cert., %)

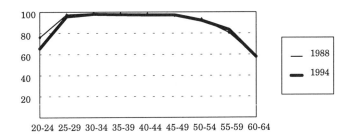

Source: Labour Force Survey

Figure 5.13: Male Labour Force Participation (by Completed Education — Third Level, %)

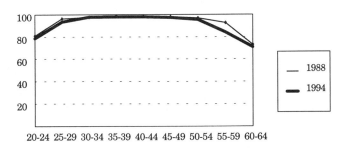

Source: Labour Force Survey

As shown in Figure 5.11, over the period 1988 to 1994 there has been a significant reduction in labour force participation by those aged 25 to 40 with only a primary education. For all other categories of males in that age group, including those with only an Intermediate Certificate, there was little change in participation over that period (Figures 5.12 and 5.13). As we shall see below, this fall in participation coincides with an increase in the unemployment rate across all age groups for males with only a primary education. This suggests that males in this category may face a growing problem of discouragement which is reflected in greater detachment from the labour force.

Unemployment

As already mentioned in Chapter 3, high unemployment has been a major contributor to Ireland's high dependency levels in the past, especially in the 1980s. Figure 5.14 shows the long-term trend in unemployment rates in Ireland and in the EU. Irish unemployment was consistently higher than the EU average in the 1980s and early 1990s. Since 1992–93, however, it has begun to move sharply downwards where the EU average has risen somewhat, with the result that Irish unemployment rates are now converging on the EU average.

Figure 5.14: Unemployment Rates in Ireland and EU15, 1960–1996 (%)

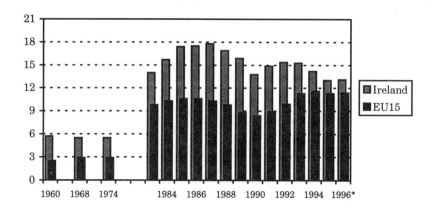

* First quarter
Source: OECD (1995a, 1996)

As we have emphasised the importance of education as an influence on labour force participation rates, we can look here at the relationship between education and unemployment in recent years. Women with only primary education have especially high rates of unemployment, particularly in younger age groups (Figure 5.15). Thus, for example, women aged 25–29 with only primary education had a 40 per cent unemployment rate in 1994, which was four times the rate for all women in that age-group. Furthermore, their unemployment rate has risen from 26 per cent in 1988. The low participation rate of poorly educated women combined with their high unemployment rate means that the proportions in work are small: in 1994, only 30 per cent of women with a primary education aged 20 to 24 were at work. For males the proportion was marginally higher at 39 per cent.

Figure 5.15: Female Unemployment (by Age, Completed Education: Primary, % of Labour Force)

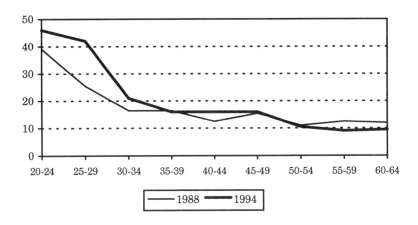

Source: Labour Force Survey

Figure 5.16: Female Unemployment (Educational Composition, %)

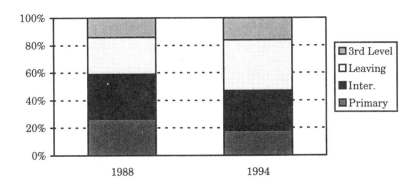

Source: Labour Force Survey

Figure 5.17: Male Unemployment (Educational Composition, %)

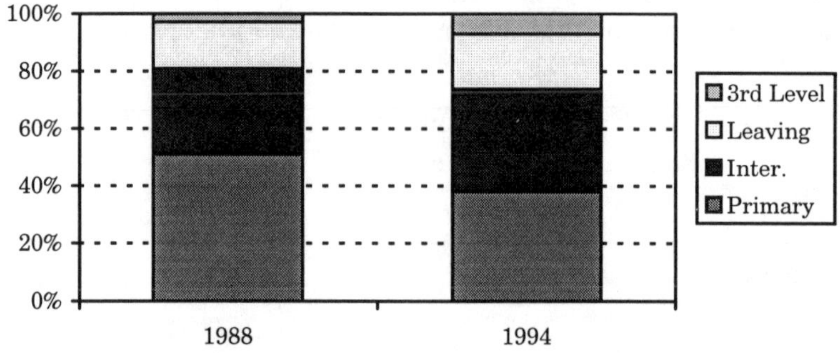

Source: Labour Force Survey

In the case of women in the younger age groups, the rise in educational attainment between 1988 and 1994 has meant that those with only primary education accounted for a declining share of the unemployed (Figure 5.16). By 1994 just over half the female unemployed had at least reached Leaving Certificate standard and around 15 per cent had third-level education. This shows a major contrast compared to the situation for males where over 75 per cent of those who are unemployed have not reached Leaving Certificate standard (Figure 5.17).

The concentration of unemployment among males with low educational attainment is even more marked than in the case of females. This to some extent reflects the fact that a much smaller proportion of females in this educational category are in the labour force, possibly because of the availability of other forms of income support, including the state support for lone parents.

Future Trends

As discussed above the participation rate for married women has risen rapidly over the last 10 years as younger women remain on in the labour force and older women in their 40s return to it. As the educational composition of the population of working age gradually changes this will be a powerful force in increasing female participation. The expected fall in fertility will reduce the number of women with children and the amount of time spent looking after children of dependent ages. Finally, continuing economic growth and growth in employment will make participation in the labour force financially attractive for women.

The result of all of these factors will be that by 2011 the labour force participation of women in the working age-groups will have risen from its current level of around 40 per cent to around 55 per cent (Figure 5.18) (Canny *et al.*, 1995). The rise would be even greater except for the fall in participation in the earlier years due to increasing time spent in education and, for older women, the trend towards earlier retirement which affects both women and men. It should be stressed that these projections are liable to considerable margins of error. The changes are taking place so rapidly that it is dangerous to project forward on the basis of current trends. Until we have a better understanding of the role of education and fertility in the participation decision we will remain very much in the dark about likely future trends. Nevertheless, it seems quite likely that the rise in participation by women in the labour force will continue and will be an important factor in the progressive reduction in the rate of economic dependency in Ireland which has been described in Chapter 3.

While the outlook for unemployment has become more optimistic in the last two to three years, considerable pessimism remains about the outlook for those who are long-term unemployed.

Figure 5.18: Female Participation Rate (Ages 15–64, %)

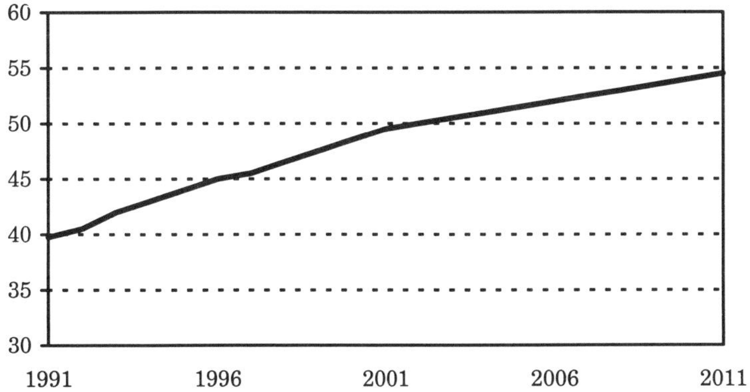

Source: Labour Force Survey

The incidence of long-term unemployment in Ireland is exceptionally high and is dominated by long-term unemployment among older men. Their employment prospects are poorer than for other groups of unemployed partly because they have been unemployed so long (employers are often reluctant to hire those who have been out of work for a long time) and partly because they find it difficult to compete in the labour market with the flood of younger, better educated workers coming onto the labour market (O'Connell and Sexton, 1994). The difficulty in absorbing this group into employment partly accounts for the expectation that unemployment will remain relatively high in the foreseeable future despite the undoubted growth in labour demand.

A final factor which will affect the economic burden which the dependent population will represent for those working is the growth in productivity of those at work. The rapid rise in the education of the labour force has already played an important role in raising the level of output and incomes in the economy. For the future it can be anticipated that this factor will continue to contribute to Ireland's rate of growth being well above the EU average, at least until the end of the next decade. This factor, which has not yet been quantified, will play an additional role in reducing the burdens on the working population over the next 20 years.

Chapter 6

Population Ageing — The Elderly

Population ageing in Ireland in the years ahead will occur partly in the form of "ageing at the base" (falling numbers of children and young adults) and partly in the form of "ageing at the apex" (increasing life expectancy and a growing number of older people). This chapter focuses on the latter aspect of population ageing, and in particular on the implications which the growing numbers of older people might have for support requirements. It first outlines key demographic trends in the elderly population, expanding on the information on this issue presented in Chapter 3. It then considers the implications of trends in the elderly population for the three major dimensions of support requirements for older people — pensions, health care and social care.

Demographic Trends in the Elderly Population

Basic data concerning the future size of the elderly population have been set out in Chapter 3 (see Figures 3.1–3.6, along with the accompanying tables in the appendix). The key projection is an increase in the population aged over 65 from 402,000 in 1991 to over 690,000 in 2026, an increase of about 72 per cent (Figure 6.1). The increase is unevenly distributed over the period in that most of it is projected to occur after 2006. Prior to 2006, the elderly population is projected to grow only to around 440,000, a modest increase of 10 per cent or so over 1991. The implications of these developments for the dependency ratio have already been considered in Chapter 3.

Figure 6.1: Projected Age-Composition of Elderly Population, 1991–2026, Thousands

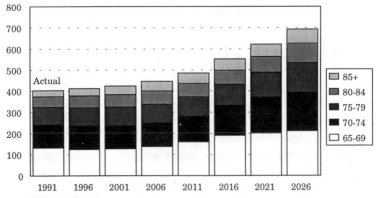

Source: CSO (1995)

Within the elderly population, the greatest absolute increase is projected to occur among the younger elderly, but the greatest relative increase occurs among the older elderly (Figure 6.2). Thus, for example, the age-group 65–69 is projected to grow by 80,000, compared to less than 40,000 among the age-group 85 and over. However, in relative terms, the increase among the 65–69 age-group, at 60 per cent, is only half that among those aged 85 and over, which is 120 per cent.

Older Age Life Expectancy

Increases in life expectancy have been one of the factors contributing to population ageing in other countries. One of the reasons for the slower rate of population ageing in Ireland has been the smallness of the increases in life expectancy at older ages which have occurred in this country. Life expectancy among older people in Ireland is now among the lowest in the western world (excluding a number of eastern European countries which recently have experienced catastrophic declines in life expectancy) (Fahey and Murray, 1994). In the early part of the present century, Ireland not only had a comparatively high overall life expectancy by the standards of the day, it also had reasonably high levels of life expectancy among older people (*General Report*, Census of Population 1926). Since then, life expectancy at birth has

Figure 6.2: Projected Increase in the Elderly Population
(by Age-Group, 1991–2026)

A. Numerical Increase by Age-Group (thousands)

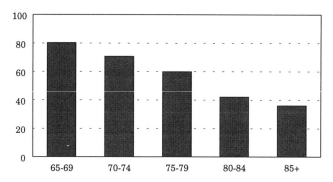

B. Percentage Increase by Age-Group (per cent)

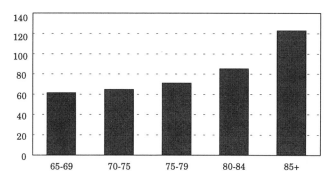

Source: CSO (1995)

increased greatly in Ireland — from 57 years in 1926 to 72 years in 1991 for males and from 58 to 78 years for women over the same period. However, by far the largest share of this increase has been due to declines in mortality in childhood and early adulthood.

Life expectancy increases at older ages have been very slight, principally because life expectancy for older men has scarcely increased at all (Figure 6.3). In 1986, life expectancy for men at age 65 (which was 12.6 years) was marginally *lower* than it had been in 1926 (when it was 12.8 years). Over the same period, life expectancy for women at the same age increased by only 1.8 years (from 13.4 in 1926 to 16.2 in 1986), a very modest increase by the standards of other countries. While mortality rates among children in Ireland are now among the lowest in the world, mortality rates among older people are comparatively high and constitute one of the more important failures in public health in this country.

Figure 6.3: Life Expectancy at Older Ages in Ireland, 1926–1991

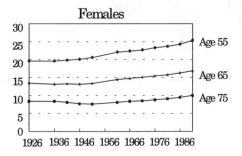

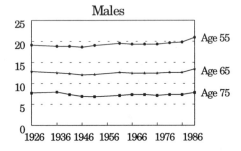

Source: Irish Statistical Bulletin, December 1995

In the period 1986–1991, older age life expectancy in Ireland increased by 0.8 of a year in the case of men at age 65 and by 0.9 of a year in the case of women at that age. For men, this was an historically novel increase (and is reflected in Figure 6.3 by the sudden upward movement at the end of the trend-lines for males) and in the case of women represented a stronger rate of improvement than had occurred previously. Death statistics up to the end of 1995 suggest that the improvements have not persisted into the 1990s at the same rate. The trends seem to have settled back to their former relatively flat course since 1991, though it will require detailed age breakdowns of the population from the 1996 Census of Population to confirm if this is so.

Marital Status

Marital status has a central bearing on the support requirements of the elderly since family members are the main sources of informal support for older people. Married elderly are likely to have spouses and/or children to provide informal care, while the widowed are likely to have children. In Ireland, the family networks of married and widowed elderly people are generally very large (Fahey and Murray, 1994), though even in western countries where such networks are smaller, they continue to be effective in providing social contact and informal care for older people (Höhn, 1994).

The situation of the never-married elderly is quite different. They have no spouses, usually no children and their networks of other close kin typically are small (Fahey and Murray, 1994). Since neighbours and friends are not usually effective substitutes for the family in providing informal care, the absence of kin is likely to make the single elderly more dependent on formal care services than are the married or widowed elderly. In the past, the single elderly accounted for a disproportionately large share of the elderly in long-term residential care (National Council for the Aged 1985, p. 23), though there is insufficient data to establish if this is still the case.

The implications of marital status for kin availability and social support for older people has been recognised in all countries but is especially important in Ireland. In 1991, 23 per cent of the population aged over 65 in Ireland was unmarried, by far the largest such proportion in any western country. This in turn reflected the low marriage rate which had prevailed in Ireland in the 1930s, 1940s and 1950s and which meant that a large share of those entering adulthood in that period failed to form procreative families of their own. The marriage rate rose sharply in Ireland in the 1960s and 1970s, thus altering the likely marital status profile of the elderly of the future.

Population projections provided by the CSO do not disaggregate by marital status, so that they provide no information on likely future trends in this area. This lack in turn reflects the absence of research on differential mortality by marital status, so that it is not possible to incorporate adequate mortality assumptions by marital status among the elderly population for projection purposes.

In the absence of any better alternative on this question, the Connell projections recently produced for the National Council for the Elderly have applied a uniform mortality assumption across all marital status categories and on that basis projected the elderly population by marital status up to the year 2011. A similar approach was used to project the future numbers of elderly persons living alone and not living alone (see Fahey, 1995 for details). Because of the undifferentiated character of the mortality assumptions used in these projections, the results must be regarded as crude and as more liable to error than the usual projections for age/sex groups. Nevertheless, they have value in indicating the likely overall shape of future developments in the marital status and household composition of the elderly population, even though they do not go beyond the year 2011.

These projections suggest that the carry-over effect of the improved marriage rates of the 1960s and 1970s will be substantial and will mean that the largest increases in the elderly population up to 2011, both in absolute and relative terms, will occur among married men and women. There will be substantial increases also among the widowed. The absolute number of single elderly men will change little, but the number of single elderly women will decline a good deal (Figures 6.4 and 6.5). The overall result will be a sharp decline in the proportion of the elderly population who are single, with most of the relative increase taking place among those who are married.

The percentage of elderly people living alone is projected to grow by only a modest amount — from 24 per cent in 1991 to 26 per cent in 2011 (Figure 6.6). The slow rate of growth in the propensity to live alone among older Irish people is largely the outcome of the changes in marital status composition of the elderly population just noted. The increase in the number of widowed and in the likelihood that the widowed will live alone is almost fully counterbalanced by the increase in the number of couples and the decrease in the number of single persons.

Figure 6.4: Marital Status of Elderly Population, by Sex in 1991 (Actual) and 2011 (Projected)

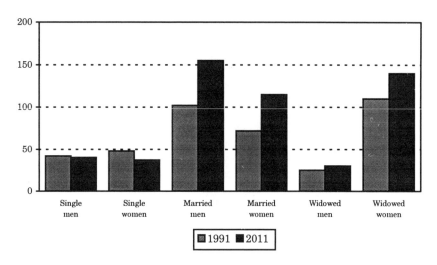

Source: Connell Projections in Fahey (1995), p. 39

Figure 6.5: Elderly Living Alone, by Sex and Marital Status, 1991–2011, % change

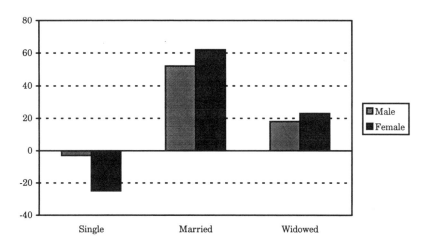

Source: Connell Projections in Fahey (1995), p. 40

Figure 6.6: Percentage of Elderly Living Alone, by Age Group, %

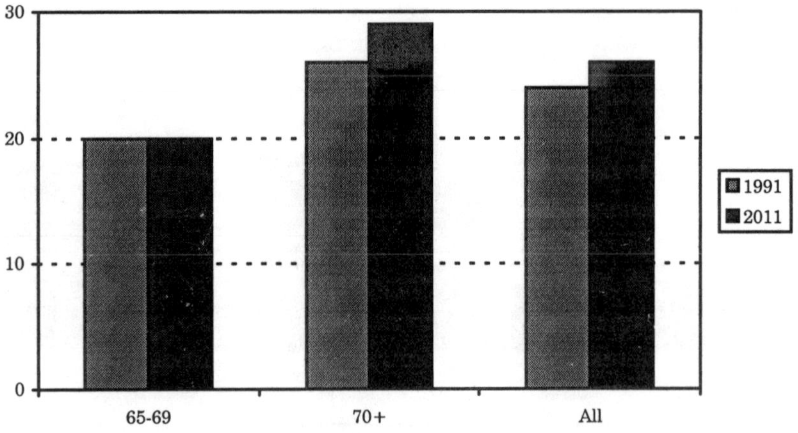

Source: Connell Projections in Fahey (1995), p. 40

Implications for Pensions

In considering the implications for the pensions system of demographic trends in the elderly population, the Final Report of the National Pensions Board, *Developing the National Pensions System* (1993) provides a useful point of departure. That report includes a projection of the costs of current social welfare provisions up to the year 2035, which in turn is based on a projection of the population and of the number of social insurance contributors over the same period (National Pensions Board, 1993, pp. 37–47, 243–248). The picture presented in the Board's report is quite pessimistic. It forecasts a large increase in the numbers of old people up to 2035, coupled with an eventual decline in the numbers of people at work and of working age. In the case of the numbers of people of working age, for example, it projects a small short-term increase followed by a long slow decline to a level in 2035 below that which prevailed in 1991. All these projections taken together mean that the Board projects a sharp increase in the proportion of the elderly relative to the support base of people in the active ages.

The central conclusion which the Board draws from its analysis is that *"the cost of providing pensions for an increasing elderly population will be borne by reducing numbers of the economically active*" (ibid., p. 39, emphasis in original). It forecasts that population change alone will give rise to a 90 per cent increase in the costs of social welfare pensions up to 2035, while the population of social insurance contributors will fall over the same period by a small amount. The report concludes that these trends raise "serious questions about the capacity of the present financing arrangements to meet these emerging costs" (ibid., p. 47). More generally, fears about the long-term sustainability of present pension arrangements causes the report to advocate a cautious approach to future improvements in the social welfare pensions system (ibid., p. 85). These fears account in part for the Board's rejection of the proposal for a universal, flat-rate, non-means-tested pension in place of the present dual system of insurance-based and social assistance pensions (ibid., pp. 96–98).

The conclusions of the National Pensions Board on these questions provide a good example of a gloomy view of Irish demographic trends and their implications for support requirements which has been referred to earlier in the present report. The analysis underlying these conclusions has already drawn some critical comment from other quarters (Hughes, 1996; see also MacCarthy, 1995; Walsh, 1996). Here we are concerned with the discrepancy between the Board's forecasts in this area and the more optimistic view of the same issues presented in Chapter 3 above. The argument in Chapter 3 is that demographic pressures on support provision are likely to ease rather than increase over the next 30 years, and are certainly unlikely to reach the same pitch as they did at various points between the 1960s and the late 1980s. How can we reconcile this optimistic prognosis with the quite pessimistic forecasts of the National Pensions Board as far as state pensions are concerned?

The answer lies principally in the exceptionally bleak nature of the population and labour force projections made by the National Pensions Board (1993, Table 4 and Table 6). The Board's projection for total population diverges sharply from that of the CSO in 1995 — where the CSO forecasts a steady increase from 1991 onwards, the National Pensions Board forecasts a steady decline (Figure 6.7, panel A). This in turn reflects the very high emigration assumptions adopted in the National Pensions Board projections (these included an assumption that net emigration would total 325,000 between 1991 and 2006). Recent developments have proven these assumptions to be quite wrong in the short term. As already noted, even the more positive forecast of the CSO, which was based on much lower emigration assumptions, is proving to have underestimated recent developments in population and labour force growth (see pp. 8–9).

Though projecting an overall population decline, the National Pensions Board forecasts an increase in the elderly population which is almost in line with that of the CSO[1], meaning that the National Pensions Board projects a more rapid ageing of the population than does the CSO (Figure 6.7, panel B). The National Pensions Board also projects a poor performance in the size of the workforce whose taxes and social insurance contributions form a major funding source for social expenditure. The Board's projection model assumed that the unemployment rate would remain constant at the 1992 level up to 2035. In fact, unemployment (measured on a Labour Force Survey basis) fell from 15.5 per cent in 1992 to 12.7 per cent in 1995, and is projected to fall to 11.0 per cent in 1998 (Baker *et al.*, 1996). A recent Forfás/ESRI projection assumes that an unemployment rate of 6 per cent is attainable by 2010 (Forfás, 1996).

The National Pensions Board's projections also assumed that the labour force would grow only slowly up to 2015 and thenceforth decline slightly below the level of the early 1990s (National Pensions Board, 1993, p. 41). In fact, the total labour force grew by about 110,000 (8 per cent) between 1990 and 1995 alone, and is projected to grow by a further 70,000 by 1998 (Baker *et al.*, 1996). There is no basis at present to assume that a decline in the labour force will set in at any time within the term for which projections of the labour force can reasonably be made.

---

[1] The lower forecast for the elderly population by the National Pensions Board reflects its reliance on mortality data from the early 1980s as the source for its mortality assumptions (National Pensions Board, 1993, p. 245). These data did not reflect the sharp and historically novel improvement in older people's mortality which occurred after the mid-1980s (see above) and as a result led to an underestimate of the growth in the elderly population which occurred since 1986.

Figure 6.7: Comparison of Projections

A. Total Population (thousands)

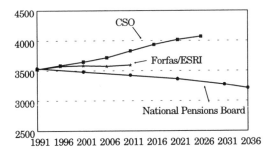

B. Elderly Population (thousands)

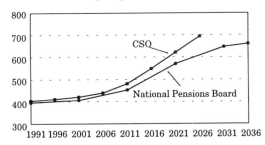

C. Workforce indices (1991=100)

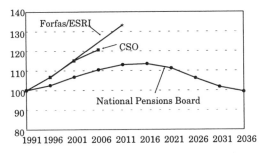

CSO = total labour force   Forfas/ESRI = employment
National Pensions Board = Social insurance contributors

Sources: CSO (1995, M1F1 assumptions); National Pensions Board (1993, Tables 4 and 6); Forfás (1996, Table 3 S3.1, S4.1)

Panel C of Figure 6.7 compares various indicators of the future trend in the size of the workforce — the National Pensions Board forecast of the trend in the number of social insurance contributors compared to the CSO's projection of the trend in the labour force projected and a recent Forfás/ESRI forecast of the trend in the numbers in employment (Forfás, 1996). Because of the conjectural nature of long-term projections of labour supply and demand, the CSO and the Forfás/ESRI forecasts on these issues extend only to the medium term (2006 in the case of the CSO, 2010 in the case of Forfás/ESRI; the longer term projections of social insurance contributors reported by the National Pensions Board must be regarded as highly speculative). Even in the medium term, as the graph shows, the National Pensions Board forecasts are considerably more pessimistic than those of the CSO and Forfás/ESRI. More recent labour force data support the general trend of the projections made by the CSO and Forfás/ESRI and diverge from those of the National Pensions Board. If the former forecasts have erred, it is at present more likely that they have erred on the side of caution rather than of optimism (see, e.g., Baker *et al.*, 1996, pp. 28–29).

In addition to what now appears as an unwarranted pessimism in its forecasts of population and labour force trends, the National Pensions Board's judgement on the future sustainability of social welfare pensions is influenced by the actuarial character of its approach. The actuarial approach, which is usually applied in a private pensions context and is quite appropriate in that context, views pensions as a closed system within which liabilities and resources have to be kept in proper balance with each other, both now and for the lifetimes of present and future beneficiaries. The sustainability of any particular set of pension arrangements can be assessed by reference to the balance (or lack of it) between resources and liabilities, in the long-term future as well as for the present.

The social policy approach to social welfare pensions is necessarily quite different. From a social policy point of view, pensions are but one element of a much larger system of social security, the purpose of which is to promote social equity and protect citizens from the vicissitudes of the market. The relationship between resources and liabilities within that system is neither closed nor inflexible over time. The number of beneficiaries, the levels of benefits they receive and the share of current revenues to be devoted to pension payments are not defined by private contract but are matters of public policy which can be altered at any time. The resource constraints on such policy changes (apart from political or other constraints) are not a direct consequence of accumulated resources and liabilities in a pension fund but are shaped by a wide range of factors — economic growth, growth in productivity, trends in overall public revenues and expenditure, trends in the size of the social security budget and in the competing claims on that budget from other welfare-dependent groups such as the unemployed, children, lone parents, the sick and disabled, etc. In order to make realistic forecasts of the future sustainability of any particular set of social welfare pensions arrangements, it would be necessary to devote as much attention to trends in these conditioning factors as to trends in social welfare pensions in a narrow sense.

The present study has attempted to take some of these conditioning factors and complexities into account even though it has not had the scope to devise a formal forecasting model along the necessary lines. It has thus ranged over issues which the National Pensions Board did not touch upon but which nevertheless seem to have a major bearing on the future sustainability of social welfare pensions. It has thus taken a more inclusive, if necessarily unsystematic, view of support requirements for children and the unemployed as well as the elderly, taking account of support provision through the family and the market as well as through the state. The trade-offs and counter-balancing effects which arise from these interacting trends give rise to a more positive long-term picture as far as pensions are concerned than that provided by the National Pensions Board: it is quite possible for pressures on the state pension system to increase while overall support requirements decline or remain stable.[2] In consequence, even if the

---

[2] Thus, for example, the social welfare pensions bill for the elderly in 1995 amounted to almost the same as the bill for social welfare payments to the unemployed (at just about £1,000m each). Future increases in the former could well be counter-balanced by reductions in the latter so that the change in the total would be modest.

Board's pessimistic outlook on pensions were justified, it need not be wholly incompatible with the more optimistic overall outlook adopted in the present report.

It may well turn out that the pessimistic scenario projected by the National Pensions Board will come to pass and that as a result the state pensions system for the elderly will eventually experience the kinds of pressure envisaged by the Board. However, alternative, more benign scenarios would seem to be much more plausible. This is particularly so for the next fifteen years or so, the maximum time-span for which forward projections of the numbers at work (the pensions support base) can reasonably be made. This means that increases in the number of pensioners would *not* be such as to greatly pressurise the social security system, since those increases would be counter-balanced by declines in the costs of unemployment and child support, as well as by an expansion in the labour force and in the number of contributors to the social insurance fund.

In the longer term, it is quite possible, though by no means certain, that trends would turn in a negative direction, principally because of the ageing of the "baby-boom" generation of the 1970s and 1980s. However, the extent of the negative turn, if it is to materialise at all, is quite uncertain, since it depends on the migration and reproductive behaviour of those yet unborn, and on the state of the economy in forty to fifty years time. All that we can say is that, given the strength of the likely intervening improvement, it would take a decline of extreme proportions to produce the degree of strain on the support system which was experienced in Ireland in the 1980s. As far as these issues are concerned, therefore, the long-term future has a less threatening appearance than the recent past.

The Elderly and Health Care

At first sight it seems obvious that an increase in the elderly population should have serious implications for health service expenditure, since older people are heavy users of health services. In Ireland, for example, persons aged over 65 have more than twice as many GP visits per year as the population as a whole, and the usage of health services generally tends to be particularly high among those aged over 75 (Nolan, 1991). It would seem obvious therefore that as the population ages, and in particular as the proportion of the population aged over 75 increases, the demands on the health services would increase accordingly. The Working Party on Services for the Elderly (1988) concluded as much when it said that "the growth in the elderly population will increase demand for health services . . . and must be a major influence on the planning of these services in the future" (p. 36).

On closer inspection, however, it is not at all clear that demographic trends have a substantial impact on health expenditure. Health expenditure has proved in the past to be determined more on the supply side than on the demand side of the health system and to have been determined especially by the pattern of economic incentives facing health service providers (Oxley and MacFarlan, 1995). To the extent that the demand side does have an effect on health service provision, the influences have as much to do with the purchasing power of health service consumers as their age or state of health (thus, for example, the extension of health insurance coverage is a major factor in the increase in demand for health services). The demographic influence is comparatively weak: health service expenditure has not been found to be consistently related to any major aspect of population structure, not even to such apparently relevant population characteristics as the size or proportion of the population aged over 75. It is, however, closely related to level of economic development as measured by per capita income and expenditure indicators (see Fahey, 1995 for an overview of the evidence). Recent experience in Ireland confirms this pattern. Trends in health expenditure in Ireland in the 1980s showed no consistent connection with demographic trends. Expenditure and consumption patterns, in fact, sometimes moved in the opposite direction to that predicted on the basis of demographic trends (Fahey, 1995, pp. 53–56). Furthermore, although Ireland in the 1980s had one of the youngest populations in the developed world, it devoted a somewhat higher share of national resources to health care than one would expect for a country at its level of national income (ibid.).

This is not to assert that demographic trends such as population ageing have no influence whatever on health expenditure but to suggest rather that the demographic effect is of a much lesser order of magnitude than such things as changes in the structure of the health services themselves and in the purchasing power of patients. The close relationship between health spending and economic growth means that we can expect health spending to rise steadily in Ireland over the coming years, just as it has tended to do over recent decades. Population ageing may add an extra impetus to that upward trend, though the extent of that additional impetus is hard to determine and in any event is likely to be small. This is so not only because the rate of population ageing in Ireland is relatively slight, but also because the effect of population ageing on health spending generally tends to be weak. While it would be wrong for health planners to ignore the effect of population ageing on health spending entirely, it would be equally unhelpful to pay excessive attention to that effect to the neglect of the numerous and more potent effects arising from other sources.

The Elderly and Social Care

If the evolution of health service provision appears to be influenced only slightly or not at all by demographic developments, the same may not be true of social care services.[3] The frail elderly account for a large share of those in need of social care and there is likely to be a stronger relationship between population ageing and the growth in the numbers of frail elderly. Increased life expectancy may well enhance overall health in later life, so that the increase in the numbers of older people may not be matched by a *pro rata* increase in the numbers of frail and dependent elderly. Nevertheless, it seems likely to be associated with some increase

---

[3] The boundary between social care and medical treatment is not always easy to define precisely, since many medical services have a caring as well as a curing function. Nevertheless, the two fields are broadly distinguishable. Most social care takes place in the cared-for person's home or, failing that, in an institutional setting which is a substitute for home for those who have become too dependent to live in the community. It is therefore an extension of the home and the functions of the home rather than of the hospital or the doctor's surgery. It quite often has a medical component but it is likely to be dominated by a range of personal and social services which can be and usually are provided by non-medical personnel, including family members. These services include personal hygiene, domestic services (cooking, cleaning, shopping), household maintenance, social support (visiting, companionship, dealing with the authorities) and surveillance (reducing risks by keeping an eye on vulnerable people).

in the numbers with less severe disabilities and dependencies. This is especially so among the very old, the category of older people which, as we have seen, is increasing most rapidly in Ireland (for the international situation, see Sundström, 1994). Demographic developments therefore could well have a strong effect on the size of the population pool which is at a high risk of being in need of social care.

As in the case of pensions, however, the sustainability of the support requirement arising out of future population ageing depends not only on the numbers of those in need of support but also on the numbers available to provide support. Social care traditionally has been an informal family function. Spouses and children (especially daughters) were the usual sources of care for dependent older people. Demographic trends can have an influence on the capacity or willingness of families to provide that care. Today, emphasis is often placed on trends which indicate that family support for older people is declining. The decline in family sizes, the rapid increase in the numbers of old people living alone and the increasing labour force participation rate among women (which means that women are not available to provide care to older relatives) are among these trends.

However, there are other indications that family support for older people remains as strong and as effective as ever (Sundström, 1994). Older people maintain regular contact with non-resident family members, improved transport and communication make such contact more feasible, and the decline in the marriage rate in recent years means that many young and middle-aged adults are more rather than less available to tend to older relatives (Macunovich *et al.*, 1995). As Evason and Robinson (1996, p. 49) say, "all the evidence indicates that, far from withdrawing from caring in favour of an all-pervasive welfare state, the family remains the most important source of support for elderly persons". Other trends which are often assumed to weaken the capacity of the family to care for older people, such as the increased participation of married women in the labour force, also turn out on examination not to have any clear effect in that direction: there is "little evidence to support the hypothesis that women working outside the home are less likely to provide care to an elderly parent" (Grundy, 1995, p. 10).

Positive developments in family support are particularly relevant in the Irish case. As we saw earlier in the present chapter,
exceptionally high proportions of older people in Ireland up to
now (of the order of one in five in 1991) have never married and
are childless. These people have little or no substitute kin to provide them with effective family networks. They form a strong contrast with the majority of older people in Ireland who have large,
strong family networks and for whom social relationships within
those networks are a central part of life (Fahey and Murray,
1994). This leads to the problem of *mal-distribution* of the social
resource which families represent in the elderly population —
most older people have a great deal of that resource but a large
minority have little or none.

Demographic trends are likely to reduce that mal-distribution
in the future, especially in the short to medium term. The greatest increase in the elderly will occur among the married and widowed, while the single elderly population is projected to decline
slightly in absolute terms and more substantially in relative
terms up to 2011 (see Figures 6.4 and 6.5). As a result, spouses
and children will be more rather than less available as sources of
social care for older people. Family networks may become smaller
on average because of falling fertility but such things as the number of adult children which old people have is less important than
the presence of at least one child in guaranteeing social support
for old people (Grundy, 1995). In addition, in Ireland, falling emigration might well mean that family members are more likely to
be close at hand. In short, present trends indicate that the incidence of family-less older people will decline, leading to a major
improvement in the distribution of the family as a social resource
among the elderly population.

Thus, although demographic and social changes may affect the
supply of relatives available to care for older people, many of
these changes will be positive rather than negative. This is especially true in Ireland where the supply of relatives for older people was mal-distributed in the past and is likely to be more evenly
and more widely distributed in the future. There is thus no reason to expect from demographic trends that the balance between
social care requirements for older people and the capacity of
families to provide that care will worsen in the years ahead. If

anything, some improvement in that balance is quite plausible, at least for the generations who formed their families in the period from the 1960s to the 1980s and who will be entering old age in the early decades of the next century.

The increase in the numbers of older people will give rise to additional demand for formal social care, both non-residential and in residential institutions for the dependent elderly. Some of this demand is likely to be met through the market, as older people or their families purchase social care services. Some is likely to be met through social provision, as reflected for example in the recent rapid expansion of the home-help service which is funded by the Health Boards (Lundström and McKeown, 1994). The mix of private and public provision in this area, as in other areas, will be determined by public policy and the evolution of market demand and provision rather than by demographic trends. As far as the sustainability of the resulting financial burdens on public spending are concerned, the same considerations arise as in the case of pensions. Because of labour force growth and declining unemployment, the financial support base for social services for the elderly is likely to widen in tandem with the increase in the financial burden so that the existing balance between the two is unlikely to be radically altered by demographic trends.

Conclusions

In Chapter 2, it was suggested that population ageing, as represented by the decline in the numbers of children and the rise in the numbers of older people, is likely to give rise to a shift in the composition of the support requirement. Since the support of children is largely a private family responsibility while the support of older people is much more a public responsibility, a decline in the former and in increase in the latter will mean that the share of the total support requirement which is provided by the family will reduce while the share provided by the state will increase. The present chapter has further examined the scale and extent of the increase in state provision which will be required by the increase in the numbers of older people, with particular reference to the implications for social welfare pensions, health care and social care.

The central conclusion is that the additional burden on public spending which will arise from the growth in the elderly population should be quite manageable and gives no cause for alarm about the sustainability of social welfare pensions, health services or other social services for older people for the foreseeable future. This conclusion is based on the expectation that the active population and the labour force will grow and the numbers of unemployed will decline in the years ahead. Reduction in the present massive burden of payments to the unemployed coupled with an increase in the tax and social insurance base caused by labour force growth will greatly enhance the capacity of the state to meet its obligations to older people. Other developments such as the fall in the numbers of children may have effects in the same direction. As a result, while growth in the number of older people will undoubtedly give rise to an increase in financial burdens on the state, parallel developments in the active age ranges will enhance the state's ability to carry those burdens. As a result, the overall balance between support requirements and support resources is unlikely to be radically altered as far as public provision for older people is concerned.

The longer term problems arising from the ageing of the large cohort of young adults of today could be real, but it is easy to be excessively pessimistic on that score. That eventuality is so far away and will be influenced by such a host of unpredictable factors that it is idle to speculate about the precise level of dependency burdens in forty to fifty years time. To do so is to second-guess the behaviour of generations yet unborn, as well as the long-term fate of the economy. In so far as we can look that far into the future, the outlook is much less unrelievedly problematic in Ireland than is often suggested. There may be some worsening of dependency burdens in the long term, but the intervening improvements will mean that, relative to the present position, the outcome will still be more favourable than we have now.

Chapter 7

Summary and Conclusion

The purpose of this study has been to examine the likely impact of future demographic trends on welfare and income support requirements in Ireland. The study has not had the scope to develop formal quantitative models for this purpose. Rather, it has aimed to assess in a discursive way the interactions between different aspects of demographic trends — such as the decline in the numbers of children combined with the increase in the numbers of older people — as influences on welfare and support requirements. The purpose of the present chapter is to summarise the main findings of the study and draw out the implications for policy.

Key Issues

The study has distinguished two aspects of support requirements which may be influenced by demographic trends. The first is the *overall level of support* associated with the dependency structure of the population (i.e. the balance between productive and dependent segments of the population, however the terms "dependent" and "productive" may be defined). In Ireland as elsewhere, the concern has been expressed in recent years that certain demographic trends, such as the ageing of the population and the growth of lone parenthood, may worsen the dependency balance and lead to rapid growth in the overall level of support which is required. The present study has provided a critical examination of these concerns in the Irish case.

The second key issue has been the *composition of support provision* which may exist within any given overall level of support. Even in cases where demographic trends may have only limited impact on the overall level of support, they may cause major shifts in the distribution of support between types of support provision. Three main types of support can be distinguished on the basis of the channels through which they are provided — the family, the market and the state. Some commentators have argued that, whatever about trends in overall levels of support, the share of the total which falls on the *state* could become unsustainably heavy and could jeopardise the future of the income support systems and social services which have grown up in western welfare states in the last half-century. The study has examined the extent to which concerns such as these can validly be applied to Irish circumstances over the next thirty years or so.

Trends in Overall Support Requirement

Falling Dependency Levels

Much of the concern about demographic "crises" in western countries has arisen from worsening dependency trends. Ireland is in an unusual position in that its dependency levels are improving and are likely to be lower in thirty years time than they were at various points in the last thirty years (see Chapter 3). Since the 1960s, Ireland has had dependency levels that were extraordinarily high by the standards of other western countries. In the early part of that period, Ireland's high dependency was caused mainly by the contraction in the active population as a result of young-adult emigration in the 1950s, coupled with a moderately high fertility rate and an elderly population that was large by the standards of the time. By the 1980s, the active population had recovered in size (partly because of return migration among those who had left in earlier decades), even though the child population had also grown rapidly. However, apart from a brief favourable period in the 1970s, dependency remained exceptionally high because of a combination of high unemployment and low labour force participation rates within the population in the active ages.

The mid-1980s witnessed peak levels of *economic* dependency (the ratio between workers and dependants). At that time, a small work force was supporting a very large child population, a very large number of unemployed and a reasonably large elderly population. The number of women in home duties was also very large. The majority of these should be counted as economically productive rather than dependent and as important providers of support within families. However, as an informal economic activity, housework is untaxed and does not contribute directly to public revenues. In addition, it is likely that a certain proportion of women in home duties were underemployed or a source of hidden unemployment.

The trend in economic dependency began to turn in a positive direction in the mid- to late 1980s. While the numbers of elderly grew, other major categories of dependants — especially children and (after 1993) the unemployed — declined. At the same time, the numbers at work began to grow, so that the dependency balance improved considerably. This positive trend is likely to continue, especially over the next ten to fifteen years, so that economic dependency will be markedly lower in the next decade than at any time since the 1960s. At the peak of economic dependency in the mid-1980s, there were over 220 dependants for every 100 workers. According to the recent Forfás/ESRI projections, that ratio will have fallen to 133 dependants per 100 workers by the year 2010 (Forfás, 1996, Tables S3.1, S4.1). Even though a certain degree of population ageing is likely to have occurred over that period, labour force growth will also mean a slight decline in the number of *elderly* dependants per 100 workers — from 35 in 1986 to 31 in 2010.

The combination of unfavourable conditions which created the extreme dependency levels of the 1960s through to the 1980s are now passing away and are unlikely to recur in as extreme a form at any point over the next three decades. Ireland is thus now moving into a new era of easing dependency burdens, no matter how those dependency burdens are defined or measured. On the basis of the forecasts of the age-structure of the population used in the present study, the improving trend in dependency in Ireland may last only up to the middle or end of the next decade and then may begin to reverse in a negative direction. However, the slowness in the negative age-dependency trend in the second decade of the next century, and the healthier base position from which it will then be starting out, mean that dependency levels in thirty years time are forecast to be lower than those being experienced at present and are likely to be considerably below those of the recent past. In addition, more recent data suggest that available forecasts may have under-estimated the strength of population growth in the years ahead, mainly because they did not anticipate the extent to which emigration has fallen off. Revised

forecasts may indicate that if trends are to turn in a negative direction in the years ahead, the negative turn may be further away
and less severe than the projections used in the present study had
forecast. This again reinforces the view that even in the long-term
future, the outlook as far as dependency is concerned is a great
deal more favourable than the record has been over recent decades.

The Role of Unemployment

If there is a doubt about the favourable character of dependency
trends over the next thirty years, it arises less from demographic
movements in the narrow sense (changes in the size and age
structure of the population) than from trends in the economy, especially as reflected in the level of unemployment. The population
in the active ages will be *available* in sufficient numbers to provide the support base for dependent groups, but it is not clear if
the economy will be capable of utilising the resource which they
represent.

It is unrealistic to attempt long-term predictions of future unemployment levels. However, the very high unemployment levels
of the late 1980s and early 1990s have declined rapidly since 1993
and are projected to continue to do so well into the next century.
One recent projection has forecast a halving of the present unemployment rate to 6 per cent by the year 2010 (Forfás, 1996).
The large corps of long-term unemployment which is present
within overall unemployment presents the greatest obstacle to
reductions in unemployment, though it remains to be seen
whether policy measures combined with buoyant labour demand
can remedy this problem. Even in the event that unemployment
fails to decline as expected, other developments such as an increase in the size of the labour force will mean that economic dependency is unlikely to be as high in the decades ahead as it was
in the last decade.

Comparisons with Other Countries

Many western countries are now becoming worried about the dependency levels they may experience in the future as a result of
demographic trends. In an Irish context, the point to note about
such concerns is that they are much more a matter of the past

rather than of the future. Ireland in the 1980s has already experienced a dependency scenario which was more extreme than that which other countries fear may now lie before them. It would require an unlikely combination of high unemployment, resurgent fertility and continuing rapid growth in the elderly population to raise economic dependency levels in other European countries to the level experienced in Ireland in the mid-1980s. If those countries wish to imagine what high dependency looks like and what effects it might have on living standards, public expenditure and so on, they need look no further than Ireland in the 1980s for an illustration. The improvement in Ireland's dependency levels which is now emerging serves simply to bring Ireland back into line with the dependency levels which have been common in other countries in the recent past, and in that sense there is nothing unusual in those levels. However, the timing of Ireland's downward movement in dependency is exceptional since it coincides with a period of general upward movement in dependency in other countries. Thus, it is the *direction* of present trends in dependency in Ireland, rather than the level of dependency, which is distinctive by comparison with other countries.

Trends in Kinds of Support Required

Given that overall dependency levels in the decades immediately ahead are likely to be more favourable than those of the decades just gone by, the focus of concern for the future shifts to the *composition* of dependency and of the support requirements which go with it. The key question here is the changing distribution of support requirements across the three main channels of support provision — the family, the market and the state — and in particular the extent to which demographic trends will throw a disproportionate share of the overall support requirement onto the state.

A number of conflicting tendencies are evident in the family–market–state mix of support provision: population ageing will tend to shift the support burden from the family to the state, but other trends (labour force growth and consequent revenue growth, falling unemployment and falling fertility) will have large compensatory effects on state spending. It is difficult to anticipate what the overall net effect of these conflicting tendencies will be. All we can do here is summarise what they will involve.

Population Ageing will Increase the Support Burden on the State

Falling numbers of children and increasing numbers of old people will lead to a major shift in support requirements from the family and the market to the state. In Ireland, as in most western countries, children are defined as primarily a private family responsibility which is met by a mixture of informal family care (provided especially by mothers) and financial provision funded by paid market work on the part of one or both parents. State provision, though dominant in certain areas such as education and health care, is supplementary rather than primary. This is so particularly in that income support for the majority of children (in the form of Child Benefit) provides for only a fraction of the actual financial cost of children, and no public provision is made to compensate for the opportunity cost of parents' childcare time.

Support for the elderly, by contrast, is defined as primarily a public responsibility — eight out of ten elderly people receive social welfare pensions, a further 7 per cent receive state occupational pensions, and seven out ten of the elderly (who are disproportionately heavy consumers of the health services) are covered by medical cards. Family support for older people, which takes the form especially of informal care for the frail elderly, accounts for a small part of total provision to the elderly as a whole (i.e. including pensions as well as health and social care). Even at that, family provision for the frail elderly qualifies for certain limited forms of state subvention.

The implication is that a decline in the numbers of children will result principally in savings for families while an increase in the number of old people will result principally in extra costs for the state — particularly in connection with social welfare pensions for the elderly. Growth in the numbers of old people does not mean that the overall support requirement will increase, but it does mean that the share of that requirement which is carried by the state will grow larger. This compositional shift in the private/public mix of support arising from population ageing will be one of the single most important effects of demographic trends on support requirements in the decades ahead.

More Workers and Fewer Unemployed will Counter-Balance Population Ageing

While the share of the support requirement falling on the state will increase as a result of the increase in the numbers of old people, the capacity of the state to carry that burden is likely to increase at the same time, principally because of an expansion in the numbers at work and a decline in the numbers unemployed. At present, unemployment costs the state about as much as old age in social welfare payments (at about £1,000 million in social welfare expenditure each, or about 6.6 per cent of GNP in total). Social welfare savings arising from a decline in the numbers unemployed could thus go a long way to counter-balancing the extra costs of social welfare pensions for the increased numbers of older people.

Even in the absence of radical declines in the numbers unemployed, the numbers at work are likely to increase. Employment has increased rapidly in Ireland since 1993 and is projected to continue doing so for the foreseeable future. This will broaden the income tax and social insurance support base from which social provision for older people might be funded so that the balance between support requirements and support resources will improve in the short to medium term. In the longer term, any deterioration in that balance which may occur is unlikely to be so severe as to fully cancel out the intervening improvements. Pessimistic forecasts about the future sustainability of social welfare pensions for the elderly in Ireland, such as those recently made by the National Pensions Board (1993), have rightly assumed that the numbers of pensioners will increase in the future but have been excessively negative about prospects for declines in unemployment and in growth of the numbers at work. They thus understate the capacity of the pensions support base to carry the burdens of future expansion.

The Impact of Falling Fertility

The favourable outlook for support resources available to the state which has just been mentioned is reinforced by the recent downward trend in fertility. The decline in the numbers of children will release large quantities of unpaid female labour for participation in the paid labour market. This increase in participation rates by women will be one of the main sources of expansion in the labour force. This effect will be reinforced by the reduction of tax expenditures on stay-at-home wives which arises from the present system of double tax-free allowance and tax bands for their employed husbands. If present income tax arrangements persist into the future, most wives moving into paid jobs to form dual-earner couples will have *all* of their income taxed at the marginal rate, thus giving rise to a disproportionately large boost to income tax revenues.

Falling fertility thus has a three-fold effect on the size and composition of the support requirement. The first, and possibly least important, is the reduction it brings about in the support requirement for children which falls directly on the state. This reduction is comparatively small, since state support for children is in general quite limited and in those areas where it is large (e.g. education), there are high levels of fixed costs which will not be dramatically affected by reductions in the numbers of children. Secondly, and more importantly, falling fertility brings about a large direct reduction in the support burden on families and thus on the adult population more generally. Thirdly, a fall in the numbers of children causes an expansion in the support resources available to the state by freeing large numbers of women to participate in the labour force and thus to become income tax and social insurance contributors. This effect is compounded in the Irish case by the income tax treatment of married couples just mentioned which means that the entry of married women into the labour force gives a disproportionate boost to state revenues.

The overall outcome is that as women reduce the total quantum of care they give to children (simply because there are fewer children there), they may not directly divert that care to other dependent groups such as the elderly. However, they could be thought of as doing so indirectly by becoming income tax and social insurance contributors, thus enlarging the revenue base from which state social spending on those other dependent groups is funded. The decrease in the support burden on families which arises from declining fertility thus feeds indirectly into an increase in the resources available to the state for the support of other dependent groups such as the elderly and unemployed.

Because of the limited nature of the present study, it has not attempted to quantify this effect, but it needs to be taken into account in assessments of the future sustainability of social welfare
provision.

The Uncertain Implications for Health and Social Care

Within the growing elderly population, the strongest impetus towards rising costs for state provision will, as already mentioned,
arise in connection with pensions and income maintenance. In
other areas, population ageing may exert less upward pressure on
state spending than is often assumed. In health care, for example,
past experience, both in Ireland and in other countries, suggests
that where population ageing occurs it has been a relatively minor influence on health expenditure (see Chapter 6). This is
largely because health expenditure is driven by supply-side factors (such as changing medical technology or changes in funding
systems) or by demand-side factors that have little to do with age
or health status among the population at large (such as medical
insurance coverage and consumers' purchasing power).

In other areas, such as social care for the frail elderly, population ageing could well lead to demand for increased provision, especially given the rapid growth in the numbers of the very old.
However, the family rather than the state is likely to be able to
absorb much of the increased support requirement in this area.
This is especially so because of the decline in the incidence of
single and childless elderly and the increase in the number of
currently married elderly which is likely to occur in Ireland. This
will mean that larger proportions of the elderly will have spouses
and children to rely on than was the case in the past.

It should be recalled here that, because of the uniquely high
incidence in Ireland up to now of single elderly with little or no
family networks, the family as a resource for older people was
badly distributed in Ireland, so that the need for state provision of
social care was higher as a result (even if it was not always ade-
quately met). Improved marriage rates in the 1960s and 1970s
will go a considerable way to remedying these defects in the distribution of family resources for older people in the future. There
may also be some improvement in the underlying health of the
elderly and thus a raising of the age at which older people typi-

cally experience serious physical decline. However, experience shows that such improvements have not greatly affected *demand* for health care one way or the other, since trends in demand are affected by many factors other than trends in health status.

We have not considered here the changing pattern of demand for social care among the frail elderly which might arise from non-demographic factors. Increases in incomes and wealth among older people, or an underlying preference not to be dependent for personal care on family members, may lead to a substitution of formal care for informal care. This in turn might give rise to policy questions about how such care might be funded, especially as between state and private provision (see O'Shea and Hughes, 1994 for a thorough discussion of the options in this area). These questions are outside our concern here since they are likely to arise independently of demographic changes, even though demographic changes may have some indirect effects.

Will Family Support for Children Decline and State Support Increase?

The decline in the size of the child population will tend to reduce the overall support requirement for children. The question remains, however, as to whether demographic trends will cause any transfer of the support burden between families and the state — will the share of that burden which is met by the state rise or decline? As with other areas of state support, there is no clear answer to this question: some aspects of demographic trends will tend to increase the level of support for children which is required from the state while others will tend to reduce it. In the absence of reliable quantification of these counter-acting trends, we can only list them rather than try to estimate their net outcome.

1. The growth in the incidence of lone parenthood will provide the main impetus towards *increased dependence* among the child population on state provision. In lone parent families, the adequacy of family transfer mechanisms is greatly reduced by the absence of the father. In some cases, fathers, though living in separate households, play a large role both in the financial support of their children and in childcare but the more common pattern is that their contributions in both these areas fall

short. The task of making good the resulting support deficit falls on the state. State supports are designed merely as a safety net for families in such circumstances, and usually are not enough to preserve the family from at least some degree of deprivation. Lone parenthood, therefore, is associated both with increased demands on public expenditure and with increased poverty among parents (especially mothers) and children.

2. The contrary possibility — that child dependence on the state will *decline* — rests mainly on the trend in unemployment. Unemployment means that the market component in family transfers fails — the money incomes from paid work which finance the family's direct financial expenditures on children are not available and have to be replaced by state transfers. Future declines in unemployment would reduce dependence among children on the state for a number of reasons: (i) claims for child dependent allowances among unemployed parents would decline; (ii) the incidence of unmarried parenthood might be reduced in that mothers would be more inclined to marry the fathers of their children if those fathers had better employment prospects and thus were likely to be able to play a useful provider role (Hannan and Ó Riain, 1993); and (iii) in cases where lone parenthood occurs, absent fathers would be more capable of providing maintenance for their children.

It is not possible to predict how strong any of these individual influences is likely to be, much less what the net effect on the private/public balance of support provision for children is likely to be. However, it is important to note that unemployment is now a major influence on the level of dependence of *children* on the state, as well as of their parents. Despite the increase in lone parenthood in recent years, therefore, it is by no means inevitable that the trend in child dependence on the state will be consistently upwards.

Economic Dependence in the Active Ages

The greatest uncertainty concerning the composition as well as the level of future support requirements arises from trends in dependence among those in the most economically active age ranges. In recent decades, such dependence has been very high in Ireland, mainly because of a combination of low labour force participation rates among women and high unemployment. Demographic factors will have a mixed effect here. The supply of young people entering the labour force will decline and the departure of older people through early retirement may increase in the years ahead. These factors will tend to reduce the size of the labour force. However, the supply of prime-age women is projected to increase rapidly, leading to net growth in the labour supply. Current demographic projections assume that labour absorption will be less than complete, in that all recent projections have built in some element of net emigration over the coming decades, while it is generally assumed also that full employment is unlikely to be achieved among those who remain in Ireland.

The Role of Education

In looking at demographic trends in Ireland and their associated dependency patterns, the influence of improved education levels in the population is ubiquitous. It is not just that stronger economic performance in recent years may be partly the consequence of the long-standing record of educational investment. It also appears that practically all demographic behaviours are influenced by education — particularly the decline in the marriage rate, the fall in fertility, the growing participation of women in the labour force and the peculiar pattern of cyclic migration which has emerged among the educated in Ireland in recent years. Rising educational attainment is still feeding through into the adult population — the first beneficiaries of free secondary education in the late 1960s are still only in their early 40s, while the products of the education boom of more recent years are still only in early adulthood. The long-term effects of rising educational levels are thus still in the making. We have tried to point to some of these effects in the present study, but it is difficult to predict how the complex interactions which arise from improved educational levels will work out in the future.

Marriage and Parenthood

The rise in unmarried parenthood in recent decades has occurred mainly among mothers aged under 25. While overall fertility among young mothers declined during the 1980s, it was marked by a sharp "retreat from marriage" — the majority of births to mothers under age 25 now occur outside marriage. Among mothers in their late twenties and thirties, by contrast, the vast majority of births occur within marriage. It also appears that many mothers who begin family formation outside of marriage in their teens or early twenties subsequently marry as they grow older. The decline in the role of marriage in family formation, therefore, is concentrated in the earliest stages of family formation and among those who begin the process at a young age. Marriage retains its traditional place in family formation among those who have their first birth after age 25. It is also important as a somewhat delayed option among those who have their first birth outside marriage at a young age. While the role of marriage in family formation is thus changing, it would be easy to underestimate its continuing significance for family life in Ireland, even among those who begin their families outside of marriage.

Unmarried Parenthood and Education

The different place of marriage in family formation among younger and older mothers just noted is probably closely related to education and the labour market prospects associated with it. Young women who leave school early have poor job prospects and thus are more inclined to become mothers at an early age. Perhaps more importantly, the fathers of their children are likely to be in similar circumstances and so may be perceived by young women as having little to offer by way of financial security — thus the reluctance among young mothers to marry them (Hannan and Ó Riain, 1993). Better educated women are more likely to defer family formation until they have secured their labour market position and are more likely to have partners who are themselves reasonably secure in jobs — and thus to be more attractive as potential husbands and supporters of children. The increasing share of well-educated women among those of marriageable age goes some way towards explaining the decline in marriage rates in recent years. Well-educated women have always had lower marriage rates, so that their growing presence in the population tends to push overall marriage rates downwards.

Education, Children and Women's Labour Force Participation

Among women, patterns of labour force participation reveal sharp differences by educational level and by presence of children, but not by marital status. Women are likely to participate if they have no children, no matter what their marital status. They are also very likely to participate if they have third level education, and it appears that this is so even if they have children. Women's labour force participation is therefore likely to increase sharply in the future, partly because of the decline in fertility and partly because of their rising educational profile. These latter two factors, of course, are also related to each other.

Policy Implications

Much of the concern which has arisen in Ireland about the effects of future demographic trends on welfare and support requirements has been imported from abroad and has been inappropriate in the Irish context. Other countries are fearful of the "demographic winter" which they face (perhaps unduly so since demography is not as deterministic as much of the alarmist comment would lead one to believe). Ireland is different in that it has already had its demographic winter — and indeed it was a uniquely long winter which lasted from the mid-nineteenth century. Spring began to break through in the 1960s but the climate of demographic dependency remained unfavourable in many ways up to the recent past. The mid-1980s brought a particularly unfavourable spell. At that time, an exceptionally small working population was supporting a relatively large population of children, old people, unemployed and underemployed. Now it seems, as we approach the end of the century, a long-term improvement in demographic dependency is on the horizon. The ratio between dependent and productive segments of the population is about to become more favourable to an unprecedented extent.

Below-replacement fertility, leading to a decline in the size of the child population, is one of the main forces behind this development (alongside falling unemployment). Paradoxically, however, population replacement is likely to work more effectively now and in the foreseeable future than it normally did in the past when fertility was high. This is so because the traditional haemorrhaging of population through emigration will be stemmed either through a reduced outflow or a greater return of past emigrants, and far larger proportions of those born in Ireland will remain and live most of their lives in Ireland.

The new demographic era may have its problematic aspects, but the contrast with the past is likely to be striking. The demographic prospect in Ireland is also in contrast with that of most other western countries. For the most part, they are now entering the downside of what has been a long upward movement, while Ireland is just emerging from a long trough.

Affordability of the Welfare State

The key policy implication which emerges from this prospect concerns the overall affordability of the welfare state in Ireland, or indeed of individual elements of the welfare state such as the system of old age pensions. The lesson which has sometimes been drawn from rising dependency levels in other countries is that the welfare state is becoming unaffordable — there will be too many dependants per worker for current levels of provision to be sustained into the future. It is not our task here to question the validity of this argument in those countries where is might have some application. Rather, our concern is to point out that the basic premise of the argument simply does not hold in the Irish case. In Ireland, exceptionally among western countries, there will be considerably *fewer* dependants per workers in the future than there have been in the recent past. By the logic of the argument made in other countries, therefore, the welfare state in Ireland should become more affordable in the years ahead than it has been at any time in the last three decades.

Old Age Pensions

It is particularly important to emphasise this point in connection with old age pensions. The extra burden on the public pension system which will be caused by ageing of the population has been frequently cited as the most unsupportable aspect of the welfare state for the future, the large extra weight that will break the camel's back. A number of factors mean that this concern does not arise in the Irish case.

One is that population ageing in Ireland is projected to be quite modest by the standards of other countries. Thirty years ago, Ireland had the highest old-age dependency ratio in the western world, thirty years hence it will have the lowest. The increase in old-age dependency in Ireland by the 2020s is projected to be of the order of a quarter, compared to a two- or three-fold increase in many other western countries.

The second factor which tends to nullify concerns about the affordability of old age pensions in Ireland in the future is the projected growth in the numbers at work. Over recent decades, and especially in the 1980s, Ireland has had an exceptionally small share of its population in employment. The population share represented by children, the elderly, the unemployed and women who, though active in home duties, were outside the tax net, was exceptionally large. Economic recovery coupled with declines in emigration, the carry-over effect of the present large numbers of young people, the increased participation by married women in the labour force and the decline in unemployment together mean that the numbers at work are projected to grow steadily over the coming years. This means that while on an age-ratio basis, old dependency will increase somewhat in the years ahead, *on an economic basis, it will actually decline.* There were approximately 35 elderly persons per 100 workers in 1986, whereas present projections suggest that this will fall to 31 by 2010. Even if the employment projections on which this forecast is based turn out to be optimistic, it is still unlikely that the number of elderly per 100 workers will show a significant increase over this period. Thus, even if the old age pension bill rises, there is an important sense in which it will be no less affordable in the future than it has been in the past.

The final factor affecting the affordability of old age pensions (and indeed of the social welfare system as a whole) is the impact on total social spending of a decline in unemployment. While there is no firm guarantee that unemployment will decline, recent indications on this front are good, and indeed it would be quite defeatist to assume that unemployment will *not* decline from the very high levels of the recent past. It has been beyond the scope of the present study to attempt to calculate the public savings likely to arise from falling unemployment but such savings are likely to form a major and positive counter-weight to the increase in the exchequer cost of old age pensions.

Any one of these three factors on its own might not be enough to allay concerns about the affordability of rising old age pensions for the future. Taken together, however, they provide a set of conditions which means that the increase in social spending arising from a growing elderly population is likely to be counter-balanced by declines in other areas or by a greater capacity in the economy to support social spending for older people. The alarms that have been raised in other countries on this question have been disputed on a number of grounds. They seem to be doubly inapplicable in the Irish case, therefore, since the underlying trends in Ireland have little of the negative character found elsewhere and have a number of positive features which at present are unknown in other countries.

Implications for Child Support

In considering the factors which might sustain the affordability of old age pensions in the future, we made no reference to the sharp decline which is projected to occur in the population of child dependants. That development could be taken as another direct contributor to the demographic dividend which would release public funds for spending in other areas (such as pensions). However, a case could be made that any public spending dividend which might result from declining numbers of children should be retained for children. Although public provision for children has been raised in recent years, present levels of child poverty are unacceptably high in Ireland and it should be a priority for social spending to raise the level of provision further in that area. The falling numbers of children make it possible to raise spending per child without increasing the total spend. It may well be both possible and necessary to raise spending per child even further and to increase the total spend accordingly. At present, Child Benefit per child is low, at approximately £7 per week (compared to £64.50 per week in the case of non-contributory old age pensions for those aged under 80 and £69.50 for those aged 80 and over). Compared to provision for old people, therefore, the level of public income maintenance provision for children is quite small, and has not been sufficient to prevent widespread poverty among children.

It is in this context of low overall provision for children that the rising incidence of lone parenthood and its implications for social spending should be viewed. There is no doubt that lone parents and their children on average have higher levels of dependence on state support than does the average two-parent family. However, the underlying problem in this context is not that provision for lone parents and their children is so high but that provision for families in general is so low. We should recall in this context that much of the child poverty which has been identified in Ireland occurs not in lone parent families but in two-parent families with large numbers of children, particularly in situations where neither parent is in a full-time paid job. It might justifiably have been argued in the 1980s that the sheer numbers of children in the country would make it difficult to sustain an adequate level of public income maintenance for families with children. The decline in the numbers of children in the future, therefore, weaken the force of that argument and make it more feasible to rectify that low standard of public provision in the years ahead.

The Influence of Support Systems on Demographic Trends

In considering the policy implications which arise from the present study, it is worth pointing out that policy in this area is more than simply a reactive adaptation to exogenously determined demographic trends. Demographic trends are themselves heavily determined by support systems, including those aspects of support which are provided by the state. Thus for example, it is quite possible that the fall in fertility which has occurred in Ireland since the early 1980s is at least partly caused by the rising cost of children and by the large share of that cost borne by families. A more generous level of support provision by the state for children (for example, through higher levels of Child Benefit or through state funding for child care services) might affect fertility trends in the future and could lead to some resurgence in fertility levels. Likewise, the somewhat more generous treatment of lone parent families compared to two-parent families in the social welfare system might well amount to a disincentive to marriage among less well-off women (McCashin, 1996). This is not to say that Lone Parents Allowances encourages pregnancy among young women or less well-off women, but for those who have become pregnant, it may well discourage marriage (thus, while the overall fertility rate among young women has fallen since the early 1980s, the proportion of that fertility occurring outside marriage has risen sharply). Social welfare provisions may thus be a contributor to the "retreat from marriage" which has accompanied fertility decline among younger women and which has given rise to the rapid increase in unmarried parenthood in recent years.

We have not attempted to trace the effects of either private or public support systems on demographic trends in the present study. Nor have we tried to factor in possible changes in state policy when considering the relationship between demographic trends and support requirements in the future. Clearly, however, the circular nature of these effects need to be kept in mind. Policy makers would need to consider not only how demographic trends might constrain or influence policy on support provision but also how policy may affect quite central aspects of demographic trends.

The Future of Social Insurance

The Department of Social Welfare has recently published a discussion document which is intended to stimulate debate on the future of social insurance in Ireland (Department of Social Welfare, 1996). That document rightly eschews alarmist comment on the future affordability of the social welfare system, including that portion of the social welfare system which is founded on social insurance rather than social assistance principles. It is mainly concerned rather with questions about the proper mix of funding and payment mechanisms which should be adopted in the future. These are issues which have not been addressed in the present report since they reflect a different set of policy concerns than those which have been the focus of the present report. Our concern here has been with the broad support implications arising from demographic trends, not with the technically most efficient mechanisms for the organisation of social welfare support within any given demographic regime.

Demographic considerations have some bearing on the issues addressed in the Department's document. However, they are more in the nature of background constraints — and fairly loose ones at that — rather than immediate determinants of what is possible and what is not. Our argument here is that, as background constraints, future demographic conditions are likely to give somewhat more rather than somewhat less room for manoeuvre in social welfare policy than in the past. However, they will not of themselves dictate what the proper choices should be in regard to the issues raised in the Department's document. Those choices will be made by reference to a wide range of technical and political questions rather than by reference to supposedly deterministic demographic trends.

Conclusion

Population decline was the outstanding symbol of Ireland's decline in the century up to 1960. It was a form of national failure for which there was simply no parallel elsewhere in the modern world. Population recovery since 1960 brought that dismal history to an end, but it initially led to burdensome age-dependency ratios and a constraint on living standards. The numbers of children soared and the numbers of elderly were relatively large for the time, while the number of working adults was depleted, first, as a legacy of the emigration of the 1950s and subsequently, in the 1980s, because of high unemployment.

It is only in the 1990s that age-dependency and economic dependency began to move in a strong, sustained and consistent downward direction. The outlook is that this favourable movement will continue for ten to fifteen years at least, and possibly longer. Some bottoming out and reversal in a negative direction may be in store in the long-term future. However, any negative turn will be on the basis of a much stronger foundation, and there is no convincing prospect, even in the long term, of anything like the dependency strains which Ireland had been accustomed to in the recent past.

Given this background, it is paradoxical that fears should be raised in Ireland today about an impending "demographic crisis" or "population time-bomb". If ever in the last two hundred years of Irish history there was a time *not* to speak of demographic crisis, it is now. For the first time in the modern era, it is possible for Ireland to look forward with some confidence to a period of well-balanced population performance combined with economic progress. While concern has been expressed in Ireland about the possible effects of population ageing, this concern is of a copy-cat variety: it is an echo of concerns which may (or may not) be valid in other countries but which have little application in the present Irish context. The policy challenge in Ireland as far as population trends and their effects on welfare and support are concerned is not so much to prepare for supposed imminent threat as to make best use of the unprecedented opportunities which are now developing.

Appendix

Tables in this appendix are presented in graphical form in Chapter 3.

Table A.1: Population and Age-Dependency Ratios, 1926-2026

Year	Population by Age-Group				Age-Dependency Ratios		
	0–14 yrs	15–64 yrs	65+ yrs	Total	Young	Old	Total
1926	867879	1832433	271680	2971992	47.4	14.8	62.2
1936	820394	1861342	286684	2968420	44.1	15.4	59.5
1946	823007	1817778	314322	2955107	45.3	17.3	62.6
1951	854810	1789392	316391	2960593	47.8	17.7	65.5
1956	860000	1700000	315000	2875000	50.0	18.0	69.0
1961	877259	1626019	315063	2818341	54.0	19.4	73.3
1966	900396	1660599	323007	2884002	54.2	19.5	73.7
1971	931152	1717277	329819	2978248	54.2	19.2	73.4
1979	1029908	1976934	361375	3368217	52.1	18.3	70.4
1981	1043729	2030722	368954	3443405	51.4	18.2	69.6
1986	1024701	2131587	384355	3540643	48.1	18.0	66.1
1991	940600	2182200	402900	3525700	43.1	18.5	61.6
1996	*841000*	*2336000*	*411300*	*3588300*	*36.0*	*17.6*	*53.6*
2001	*772900*	*2455100*	*420800*	*3648800*	*31.5*	*17.1*	*48.6*
2006	*761800*	*2518400*	*439400*	*3719600*	*30.3*	*17.4*	*47.7*
2011	*780600*	*2571200*	*479800*	*3831600*	*30.4*	*18.7*	*49.0*
2016	*791800*	*2594100*	*548200*	*3934100*	*30.5*	*21.1*	*51.7*
2021	*774100*	*2618700*	*620600*	*4013400*	*29.6*	*23.7*	*53.3*
2026	*734400*	*2640200*	*693600*	*4068200*	*27.8*	*26.3*	*54.1*

Note: Projections in italics

Source: CSO (1995) and Population Censuses.

Table A.2: Old Dependency & Young Dependency, Selected Countries, 1960 and 2020 (United Nations Projections)

	Old dependency		Young dependency	
	1960	**2020**	**1960**	**2020**
Ireland	19.4	23.4	53.9	32.6
UK	18.0	28.0	35.8	27.9
Norway	17.6	28.3	41.1	29.1
Sweden	18.1	33.9	33.3	29.6
France	18.8	31.2	42.5	27.4
Germany	17.1	31.5	31.7	19.5
Belgium	18.5	32.1	36.5	26.4
Netherlands	14.8	31.0	49.2	23.7
Spain	12.8	30.4	42.6	19.2
Portugal	12.7	26.7	46.4	24.0
Italy	14.1	36.0	37.6	18.8
Greece	12.6	34.7	40.6	21.3

Note: Projections in italics
Source: United Nations (1995)

Table A.3: Economic Dependency in Ireland and EU12

Year	Ireland		EU12
	Number of Dependants		
	Per 100 in labour force	**Per 100 at work**	**Per 100 at work**
1961	161.0	168.0	134.0
1971	168.3	183.8	146.0
1979	173.2	194.2	
1981	170.9	200.7	152.0
1986	170.7	227.7	
1991	162.7	210.9	143.0
1996	150.2	188.4	
2001	136.2	163.5	
2006	129.7	154.9	

Note: Projections in italics
Source: Labour Force Surveys and Censuses of Population; Eurostat; CSO (1995)

Bibliography

Baker, T.J., D. Duffy and D. Duggan, 1996. *Quarterly Economic Commentary*. Dublin: Economic and Social Research Institute, September.

Blackwell, John, Eamon O'Shea, Geraldine Moane and Peter Murray, 1992. *Care Provision and Cost Measurement: Dependent Elderly People at Home and in Geriatric Hospitals*. Dublin: Economic and Social Research Institute.

Tim Callan and Brian Farrell, 1991. *Women's Participation in the Irish Labour Market*. Dublin: National Economic and Social Council.

Callan, Tim, Brian Nolan and Christopher T. Whelan, 1996a. *A Review of the Commission on Social Welfare's Minimum Adequate Income*. Dublin: The Economic and Social Research Institute.

Callan, Tim, Brian Nolan, Brendan J. Whelan, Christopher T., Whelan and James Williams, 1996b. *Poverty in the 1990s: Evidence from the 1994 Living in Ireland Survey*. Dublin: Oak Tree Press.

Canny, Angela, John Fitz Gerald, Gerard Hughes, and Justin Johnson, 1995. *Implications of Major Trends for the Size, Structure and Organisation of the Workforce in 2010*, Dublin: Forfás.

Cantillon, S., J. Curtis and J. Fitz Gerald, *Medium Term Review: 1994–2000*. Dublin: Economic and Social Research Institute.

Carney, Claire, Eithne Fitzgerald, Gabriel Kiely and Paul Quinn, 1994. *The Cost of a Child. A Report on the Financial Cost of Child-Rearing in Ireland*, Dublin: Combat Poverty Agency.

Central Statistics Office, 1992. *Labour Force Survey*, Dublin: Stationery Office.

Central Statistics Office, 1995. *Population and Labour Force Projections 1996–2026*, Dublin: Stationery Office.

Central Statistics Office, 1997. *Labour Force Survey*, Dublin: Stationery Office.

Combat Poverty Agency, 1996. *Strategic Plan 1996–1998*. Dublin: Combat Poverty Agency.

Cutler, D.M., J.M. Poterba, L.M. Seiner and L.H. Summers, 1990. "An Ageing Society: Opportunity or Challenge?" *Brookings Papers on Economic Activity*, Vol. 1.

Department of Social Welfare, 1996. *Social Insurance in Ireland*. Dublin: Stationery Office.

European Commission, 1994. "Some Economic Implications of Demographic Trends up to 2020" Study No. 5, pp. 211–225, *European Economy*, No. 56.

Evason, E. and G. Robinson, 1996. "Informal Care in Northern Ireland" in R. Breen, P. Devine and L. Dowd, (eds.), *Social Attitudes in Northern Ireland*. Belfast, Appletree Press.

Expert Working Group, 1996. *Integrating Tax and Social Welfare*. Dublin: Stationery Office.

Fahey, Tony, 1990. "Measuring the Female Labour Supply: Conceptual and Procedural Problems in Irish Official Statistics", *The Economic and Social Review* 21, 2, pp. 163–191.

Fahey, Tony, 1992. "Review Article", *The Economic and Social Review* 24, 2, pp. 199–210.

Fahey, Tony, 1995. *Health and Social Care Implications of Population Ageing in Ireland*. Dublin: National Council for the Elderly.

Fahey, Tony and Peter Murray, 1994. *Health and Autonomy among the Over-65s in Ireland*. Dublin: National Council for the Elderly.

Forfás, 1996. *Shaping Our Future. A Strategy for Enterprise in Ireland in the 21st Century*. Dublin: Forfás.

Grundy, Emily, 1995. "Demographic Influences on the Future of Family Care", pp. 1–18 in I. Allen and E. Perkins, *The Future of Family Care of Older People*. London: HMSO.

Guillemard, Anne-Marie, 1991. "The Decline of Social Status? Evolution of the Welfare State for the Elderly: the Past Situation and Future Prospects", pp. 166–190 in J. Pacolet and C. Wilderom (eds.), *The Economics of Care for the Elderly*. Aldershot: Avebury.

Hannan, Damian and Seán Ó Riain, 1993. *Pathways to Adulthood in Ireland: Causes and Consequences of Success and Failure in Transitions among Irish Youth*, General Research Paper No. 161. Dublin: Economic and Social Research Institute.

Haveman, Robert and Barbara Wolfe, 1995. "The Determinants of Children's Attainments: A Review of Methods and Findings", *Journal of Economic Literature,* 33, pp. 1829–1878.

Höhn, Charlotte, 1994. "Ageing and the Family in the Context of Western-type Developed Countries", in United Nations, *Ageing and the Family,* New York: United Nations.

Hughes, Gerard, 1996. "Would Privatising Pensions Increase Savings?" *Irish Banking Review*, Spring.

Hughes, Gerard and Brendan J. Whelan, 1996. *Occupational and Pension Coverage 1995*. Dublin: The Economic and Social Research Institute.

Irish Business and Employers Confederation, 1996. *Social Policy in a Competitive Economy*. Dublin: IBEC.

Johnson, Paul, 1996. "The Anatomy of the 'Old Age Crisis'", in Peter Lloyd-Sherlock and Paul Johnson (eds.), *Ageing and Social Policy: Global Comparisons*. London: London School of Economics.

Larragy, Joseph F., 1993. "Formal Service Provision and the Care of the Elderly at Home in Ireland", *Journal of Cross-Cultural Gerontology* 8, pp. 361–374.

Leibfritz, Willi, Deborah Roseveare, Douglas Fore and Eckhard Wurzel, 1995. "Ageing Populations, Pension Systems and Government Budgets: How Do They Affect Savings?" *OECD Economics Department Working Papers No 156.* Paris: OECD.

Lloyd-Sherlock, Peter, 1996. "The Role of Public and Private Sectors in Providing Economic Support for the Elderly", in Peter Lloyd-Sherlock and Paul Johnson (eds.), *Ageing and Social Policy: Global Comparisons.* London: London School of Economics.

Lundström, F. and K. McKeown, 1994. *Home Help Services for Elderly People in Ireland.* Dublin: National Council for the Elderly.

Macunovich, D.J., R.A. Easterlin, C.M. Schaeffer, and E.M. Crimmins, 1995. "Echoes of the Baby Boom and Bust: Recent and Prospective Changes in Living Alone Among Elderly Widows in the United States", *Demography,* 32, 1.

McCarthy, Tom, 1995. "Ageing Populations and Pension Systems: Time Bomb or False Alarm?" Paper presented to Dublin Economic Workshop, October 1995.

McCashin, Anthony, 1993. *Lone Parents in the Republic of Ireland: Enumeration, Description and Implications for Social Security.* Dublin: Economic and Social Research Institute.

McCashin, Anthony, 1996. *Lone Mothers in Ireland: A Local Study.* Dublin: Oak Tree Press in association with Combat Poverty Agency.

Mjoset, Lars, 1992. *The Irish Economy in a Comparative Institutional Perspective.* Dublin: National Economic and Social Council.

National Council for the Aged, 1985. *Institutional Care of the Elderly.* Dublin: National Council for the Aged.

National Economic and Social Council, 1996. *Strategy into the 21st Century: Report No. 98.* Dublin: NESC.

National Pensions Board, 1993. *Developing the National Pension System. Final Report of the National Pensions Board.* Dublin: Stationery Office.

Nolan, Brian, 1991. *Utilisation and Financing of Health Services in Ireland.* Dublin: Economic and Social Research Institute.

O'Connell, P. and J.J. Sexton, 1994. "Labour Market Developments in Ireland, 1971–1993" in S. Cantillon, J. Curtis and J. Fitz Gerald, (eds.), *Economic Perspectives for the Medium Term.* Dublin: Economic and Social Research Institute.

OECD, 1988. *Reforming Public Pensions.* Paris: OECD.

Oxley, Howard and Maitland MacFarlan, 1995. "Health Care Reform: Controlling Spending and Increasing Efficiency". *OECD Economic Studies,* 24, 1, pp. 7–56.

O'Shea, Eamon and Jenny Hughes, 1994. *The Economic and Financing of Long-Term Care for the Elderly in Ireland.* Dublin: National Council for the Elderly.

Schulz, James H., Allan Borowski and William H. Crown, 1991. *Economics of Population Ageing. The "Graying" of Australia, Japan and the United States.* New York: Auburn House.

Sexton, J.J. and Michele Dillon, 1984. "Recent Changes in Irish Fertility", *Quarterly Economic Commentary.*

Sundström, G., 1994. "Care by Families: An Overview of Trends", in *Caring for Frail Elderly People, New Directions in Care.* Paris: OECD.

United Nations, 1995. *World Population Prospects. The 1994 Revision.* New York: United Nations.

Vincent, John, 1996. "Who's Afraid of an Ageing Population? Nationalism, the Free Market, and the Construction of Old Age as an Issue", *Critical Social Policy* 16, 2, pp. 3–26.

Walsh, Brendan, 1996. "Some Implications of the Ageing Irish Population", Department of Economics, University College, Dublin, Working Paper WP2/96.

Working Party on Services for the Elderly, 1988. *The Years Ahead: A Policy for the Elderly.* Dublin: Stationery Office.

World Bank, 1994. *Averting the Old Age Crisis: Policies to Protect the Old and Promote Growth.* Oxford: Oxford University Press.